DARK EMPATH

How To Identify Them And Lead Them Into The Light

JUDY DYER

DARK EMPATH: How to Identify Them and
Lead Them Into the Light
by Judy Dyer

© **Copyright 2022 by Judy Dyer**

All Rights Reserved.

Disclaimer: This book is designed to provide accurate and authoritative information in regard to the subject matter covered. By its sale, neither the publisher nor the author is engaged in rendering psychological or other professional services. If expert assistance or counseling is needed, the services of a competent professional should be sought.

ISBN: 979-8375536798

ALSO BY JUDY DYER

Empath: A Complete Guide for Developing Your Gift and Finding Your Sense of Self

The Empowered Empath: A Simple Guide on Setting Boundaries, Controlling Your Emotions, and Making Life Easier

The Highly Sensitive: How to Stop Emotional Overload, Relieve Anxiety, and Eliminate Negative Energy

The Power of Emotions: How to Manage Your Feelings and Overcome Negativity

Borderline Personality Disorder: A Complete BPD Guide for Managing Your Emotions and Improving Your Relationships

Empath and the Highly Sensitive: 2-in-1 Bundle

Empaths and Narcissists: 2-in-1 Bundle

CONTENTS

INTRODUCTION

Are you in a relationship with a dark empath? Do you want to know how to help a dark empath? Or do you suspect someone you know is a dark empath? If you've answered yes to any of these questions, this is exactly the right place to get the help you need. But before we get started, let me tell you a bit about myself.

I was stuck in a relationship with a dark empath for three years (his name is James and I will be referring to him a lot throughout this book) and I suffered immensely. I hadn't heard of this personality type and I didn't know how to manage his behavior, but I desperately wanted to help him. Despite how cruel he was, I saw the good in him, and I believed that if I just stuck it out, he would change. I would spend hours researching his behavior so I could understand where he was mentally, and that's when I stumbled upon the dark empath, and I knew immediately that he was one. We spoke about being empaths all the time, so I assumed I could speak to him about what I had discovered. That was the biggest mistake I could have made. One of the reasons we were drawn to each other in the first place was that we were both victims of our gift; we weren't operating at our full potential, and we weren't ready to put in the work required to achieve it. So, we coexisted as broken people, and it worked—until he started getting abusive.

When I found out he was a dark empath, I had already started my healing journey. I wanted to become who I was destined to be, and I was actively working towards it. So, when I suggested he might be a dark empath, and that by applying the strategies you are going to read about in this book he could change, he flipped out. We ended our relationship shortly after and went our separate ways.

But we met up again a few years later, and he was a completely different person; he was literally glowing, and I could feel the light radiating off him. He admitted he was a dark empath, and that he had been working with a healer who had helped him transition from the dark side into the light. His transformation lined up with the recent research conducted by Dr. Alexander Sumich and Dr. Nadja Heym from Nottingham Trent University. They found that dark empaths have just as much empathy as traditional empaths, and they are equally as capable of change as any other person suffering from a curable personality disorder.

I have said all that to say this: dark empaths can change, but it will only happen when they're ready, and it must be done on their terms. So, if you're in a relationship with or know someone who is a dark empath, don't write them off just yet—because there *is* hope. After having lived with a dark empath for three years, I've definitely got some inside information and I understand many of their unique character traits. In this book, not only will I teach you how to recognize these traits so you don't get trapped with a dark empath, I will also teach you how to help those that you know. In the following chapters you will learn:

- How to recognize a dark empath.

- The toxic personality traits of a dark empath and how to avoid them.

- Why dark empaths are prone to certain behaviors such as procrastination, perfectionism, and codependency.

- Tips on how to help your dark empath partner/friend/ loved one transition from the dark into the light.

- The mental illnesses associated with dark empaths.

- How dark empaths are prone to apathy.

Dark empaths are nuanced and complex people whom I believe have been marginalized because the world doesn't understand them. If you're in a relationship with an abusive dark empath, get out now. However, for those of you who feel there is still hope, this book is for you.

In order to maximize the value you receive from this book, I highly encourage you to join our tight-knit community on Facebook. Here, you will be able to connect and share with others in order to continue your growth.

Taking this journey alone is not recommended, and this can be an excellent support network for you.

It would be great to connect with you there,

Judy Dyer

To Join, Visit:
www.pristinepublish.com/empathgroup

DOWNLOAD THE AUDIO VERSION OF THIS BOOK FOR FREE

If you love listening to audiobooks on the go or would enjoy a narration as you read along, I have great news for you. You can download the audiobook version of *Dark Empath* for FREE just by signing up for a FREE 30-day Audible trial!

Visit: www.pristinepublish.com/audiobooks

YOUR FREE GIFT—HEYOKA EMPATH

A lot of empaths feel trapped, as if they've hit a glass ceiling they can't penetrate. They know there's another level to their gift, but they can't seem to figure out what it is. They've read dozens of books, been to counseling, and confided in other experienced empaths, but that glass ceiling remains. They feel alone and alienated from the rest of the world because they know they've got so much more to give, but can't access it. Does this sound like you?

The inability to connect to your true and authentic self is a tragedy. Being robbed of the joy of embracing the full extent of your humanity is a terrible misfortune. The driving force of human nature is to live according to one's own sense of self, values, and emotions. Since the beginning of time, philosophers, writers, and scholars have argued that authenticity is one of the most important elements of an individual's well-being.

When there's a disconnect between a person's inner being and their expressions, it can be psychologically damaging. Heyokas are the most powerful type of empath, and many of them are not fully aware of who they are. While other empaths experience feelings of overwhelm and exhaustion from absorbing others' energy and emotions, heyoka empaths experience an additional aspect of exhaustion in that they are fighting a constant battle with their inability to be completely authentic.

The good news is that the only thing stopping you from becoming your authentic self is a lack of knowledge. You need to know exactly who you are so you can tap into the resources that have been lying dormant within you. In this bonus e-book, you'll gain in-depth information about the seven signs that you're a heyoka empath, and why certain related abilities are such powerful traits. You'll find many of the answers to the questions you've been searching for your entire life, such as:

- Why you feel uncomfortable when you're around certain people

- How you always seem to find yourself on the right path even though your decisions are not based on logic or rationale

- The reason you get so offended when you find out others have lied to you

- Why you analyze everything in such detail

- Why humor is such an important part of your life

- Why you refuse to follow the crowd, regardless of the consequences

- Why strangers and animals are drawn to you.

There are three main components to authenticity: understanding who you are; expressing who you are; and letting the world experience who you are. Your first step on this journey is to know who you are, and with these seven signs that you're a heyoka empath, you'll find out. I've included snippets about the first three signs in this description to give you full confidence that you're on the right track:

Sign 1: You Feel and Understand Energy

Heyoka empaths possess a natural ability to tap into energy. They can walk into a room and immediately discern the atmosphere. When an individual walks past them, they can literally see into their soul because they can sense the aura that person is carrying. But empaths also understand their own energy, and they allow it to guide them. You will often hear this ability referred to as "the sixth sense." The general consensus is that only a few people have this gift. But the reality is that everyone was born with the ability to feel energy; it's just been demonized and turned into something spooky, when in actual fact, it's the most natural state to operate in.

Sign 2: You Are Led by Your Intuition

Do you find that you just know things? You don't spend hours, days, and weeks agonizing over decisions; you can just *feel* that something is the right thing to do, and you go ahead and do it. That's because you're led by your intuition and you're connected to the deepest part of yourself. You know your soul, you listen to it, and you trust it. People like Oprah Winfrey, Steve Jobs, and Richard Branson followed their intuition steadfastly and it led them to become some of the most successful people in the history of the world. Living from within is the way we were created to be, and those who trust this ability will find their footing in life a lot more quickly than others. Think of it as a GPS system: when it's been programmed properly, it will always take you to your destination via the fastest route.

Sign 3: You Believe in Complete Honesty

In general, empaths don't like being around negative energy, and there's nothing that can shift a positive frequency faster than dishonesty. Anything that isn't the truth is a lie, even the tiny ones that we excuse away as "white lies." And as soon as they're released from someone's mouth, so is negative energy. Living an authentic life requires complete honesty at all times, and although the truth may hurt, it's better than not being able to trust someone. Heyoka empaths get very uncomfortable in the presence of liars. They are fully aware that the vibrations of the person don't match the words they are saying. Have you ever experienced a brain freeze mid-conversation? All of a sudden you just couldn't think straight, you couldn't articulate yourself properly, and things just got really awkward? That's because your empath antenna picked up on a lie.

Heyoka Empath: 7 Signs You're a Heyoka Empath & Why It's So Powerful is a revolutionary tool that will help you transition from uncertainty to complete confidence in who you are. In this easy-to-read guide, I will walk you through exactly what makes you a heyoka empath. I've done the research for you, so no more spending hours, days, weeks, and even years searching for answers—because everything you need is right here in this book.

You have a deep need to share yourself with the world, but you've been too afraid because you knew something was missing. The information within the pages of this book is the missing piece in the jigsaw puzzle of your life. There's no turning back now!

Get *Heyoka Empath* for Free by Visiting

www.pristinepublish.com/empathbonus

CHAPTER 1:

WHAT IS A DARK EMPATH?

L ife would be so much easier if it was just black and white and there were no gray areas. But unfortunately, that's not the case! Wouldn't it be wonderful if we could look at a person and determine exactly who they are before getting involved with them? Unfortunately for empaths, we get the bad end of the stick because we are drawn to people's brokenness. That brokenness often camouflages their true character and we end up in relationships that are detrimental to our well-being. The problem with dark empaths is they are difficult to spot, and unless you are familiar with their character traits, you'll get sucked right in. In case you were wondering what a dark empath is, here is a brief description.

WHAT IS A DARK EMPATH?

Empaths are blessed with the ability to connect so deeply with the emotions of others that they can feel what others feel and experience what they experience. There's nothing better than having someone in your life who understands the very core of your being. When you're with an empath, you don't need to explain yourself or force them to see things from your point of view—because they just get it. And that's why we're attracted to dark empaths. It's definitely why I was attracted to my ex. At the beginning of the relationship, I thought it was a dream come true. He understood what it meant to be an empath. He gave me space when I needed it, had my Epsom salt bath ready when I got home from a hectic day. He knew when I had absorbed too much negative energy. I thought I'd hit the jackpot—until he started revealing his true colors. Within a few months, he started using his insight into my emotional state against me and became extremely manipulative.

Dark empaths are exceptionally calculating, and they use cognitive empathy for their benefit. There are three types of empathy, and cognitive empathy is one of them:

1. **Cognitive Empathy:** Having the ability to take on a person's perspective and thought process without an emotional attachment.

2. **Compassionate Empathy:** Having aspects of cognitive and emotional empathy where you can take on a person's perspective and experience their emotions as if you were in the same situation.

3. **Emotional Empathy:** Having the ability to feel another person's emotions so deeply that you feel as if you're having the same experience.

Dark empaths tune into emotions and suffering in the same way as empaths, but they have no sympathy for the person in question. I remember crying my eyes out in front of him, and him not even flinching. A true empath can't watch someone in pain without comforting them.

The Dark Triad and Dark Empaths

According to mental health expert Nicole Cain, one of the main traits of dark empaths is fractured empathy. Psychologically, they don't have what it takes to be fully empathetic. Fractured empathy is one of the main traits of the dark triad, which is comprised of narcissism, subclinical psychopathy, and Machiavellianism. Dark empaths are a combination of all three of these personality types.

Narcissism: Selfish or vain people are often referred to as narcissists; however, the clinical definition is a lot deeper. Psychologists make a diagnosis of narcissistic personality disorder based on the Narcissistic Personality Inventory (NPI), which is a four-part scale that evaluates how far a person will go to exploit someone for personal gain, authority, superiority, and self-absorption. The main traits of a narcissist include the following:

- They insist on being the best in all areas.

- They behave in a conceited and arrogant manner.

- They are pretentious and boastful.

- They believe everyone is jealous of them.

- They are jealous of anyone doing better than them.

- They are incapable of recognizing the feelings and needs of others.

- They get what they want by taking advantage of others.

- They monopolize conversations.

- They believe they are superior to others.

- They will only associate with people of the same social standing.

- They spend a lot of time fantasizing about power, success, beauty, brilliance, and the perfect mate.

- They expect others to see them as superior even though they haven't done anything to deserve such an accolade.

- They require excessive and constant praise and admiration.

- They live entitled lives.

- They believe in their own importance.

Subclinical Psychopathy: There is very little difference between a subclinical psychopath and a psychopath who has been clinically diagnosed (clinical psychopath). They exhibit the same behavioral patterns, except for the fact that the abnormal behaviors of a clinical psychopath penetrate every area of their lives. A subclinical psychopath seems to have some sort of control over their behavior, although it manifests every now and then. The main symptoms of a psychopath include:

- Very little empathy

- Very little remorse

- Dangerous and reckless behavior

- Criminal history, rule breakers

- Irritability and aggression

- Struggles with relationships

- Emotionally and physically abusive

- Manipulative or deceitful behavior

Machiavellianism: Although Machiavellianism is not a clinical term, this personality type is widely recognized by psychologists, therapists, and counselors. The term describes someone who is extremely manipulative, cynical, and has a tendency to lie. The main character traits of the Machiavellian personality include:

- Highly competitive
- Extremely ambitious
- Very unemotional
- Very deceitful
- Highly cynical

Although the term *dark empath* is relatively new, their character traits have been around for years and are often found in cinema and literature. These are the typical evil or mysterious characters who in the end turn out not to be so evil after all: the Mafia, who commit crimes but have a high set of moral values; the thief who makes a living by stealing but also provides for the poor; the anti-hero vampires; and the high school bad boys. One study found that, out of 991 participants, approximately 19.3% were dark empaths, which indicates that they are not as rare as experts have suggested.

If you've ever had the displeasure of being in a relationship with a dark empath, you'll know how difficult it is. A few years back, I was one of those people, and I would advise that you avoid dating them at all costs. So, let's start by identifying the different types of dark empaths you're likely to come across.

CHAPTER 2:

THE DIFFERENT TYPES OF DARK EMPATHS

D ark empaths are complex characters and they've got many different personality types. They can be drama queens, energy vampires, or manipulators—and it's important that you recognize them so you can erect your protective shield and keep them out of your life.

MANIPULATORS

Whether the manipulator in your life is a friend or a lover, manipulation is a form of emotional abuse and you should not ignore it. Here are some of the main signs that you're dealing with a manipulator:

Boundary Violations: Manipulators are expert boundary violators. Regardless of how many times you say "no," they'll do everything in their power to get what they want out of you. For example, you might tell your significant other that you don't like them going through your phone, but they keep doing it. Or you tell your friend that you don't like it when she says rude things to you in front of other people, but she keeps doing it. Boundary violation is one way in which manipulators let their victims know that their main concern is themselves.

Matching or Mirroring: We all prefer to be around people with common interests, but manipulators take it to the extreme because they want you to believe they're on your side. Pay attention to how often the manipulator listens to what you've got to say and then claims they've had a similar experience or they're currently going through something similar. When a person appears to have so much in common with you, it becomes difficult to cut ties with them because they make you feel so understood and heard. You will also find it harder to discern that they're manipulating you.

Creating a Smokescreen: Manipulators use this tactic when their victim wants to discuss something taking place in the relationship that they don't like. When you put your foot down and attempt to stand your ground and speak your mind, they will find a way to take the attention off you. For example, if you try and talk to your partner about how you feel disrespected when they gawk over the opposite sex in front of you, they will respond with something like, "Well, I'm not the one with tons of so-called work friends calling you every second when we're together! That to me is the height of disrespect! What have you got to say about *that*?" Your partner has completely dismissed your concerns and made *you* out to be the bad guy. The manipulator won't allow you to address your pain, and what they've done gets brushed under the rug.

Moving the Goalposts: This manipulation tactic makes the abuser feel unstable and unsteady in the relationship. You will never be able to please the manipulator because they are always changing their desires and requests. For example, last week your best friend said their favorite color was red so you bought them a red shirt for their birthday. When they open the gift, they look disappointed, saying something along the lines of, "It's okay but my favorite color is blue." You respond, "But you said it was red last week." And they answer, "I changed my mind yesterday." By continuously changing their expectations, they maintain control over their victim because that victim wants to make the manipulator happy. Another example is that your partner says that, in order to spend quality time together, you need to have one night a week where you both turn off your phones and chill. After a couple of weeks, they'll say one night a week isn't enough and that it needs to be two. It won't be long before they've completely isolated you from friends and family.

Making You Feel Guilty: A manipulator will guilt-trip you in order to get their own way. For example, they will keep reminding you of the times you messed up, or of how much they've helped you, so you feel you owe them something. A manipulator is highly skilled at using guilt trips to their advantage. For example, you may have arranged to go out and celebrate a friend's birthday. When you tell your partner, they'll guilt-trip you into canceling plans with your friends by reminding you of all the times you've canceled plans with *them*. They will follow that up with trying to make you feel bad because you don't spend enough time together. You'll notice that they do this anytime you want to go out with friends or family. This is another way manipulators work to isolate their victims from their loved ones.

Getting Others Involved: To manipulate their victims further, they'll get other people involved to help push their agenda. This is typically easy to achieve because manipulators are very friendly and charismatic to anyone who isn't their victim. Their partner's family and friends always love them and are shocked when they find out how abusive they are. So if they need you to do something, they'll go to your best friend or sister to persuade you. For example, you may get tired of the abuse and dump them. To get you to stay, they'll ask your friends and family to speak to you. Some people might think this is sweet and that it shows how much they like you.

Focusing on Your Insecurities: Your friends and the person you're in a relationship with often know you better than your own family members do. They know all about your insecurities, fears, and flaws, and they'll use them against you. If someone compliments your hair, they'll say something like, "But look at her big nose, though," knowing full well you've always been insecure about your nose. They'll attempt to laugh it off as a joke, but the damage has already been done. Or they'll give you a backhanded compliment and say something like, "I love your outfit; it doesn't make you look so fat." They say things like that because they know you won't pay attention to the compliment, but the insult.

THE NEGATIVE NANCY/NIGEL

Do you have a friend or a partner who never has anything good to say? They are literally one big ball of negative energy, and as an empath, you can feel their gloomy presence when they're halfway down the street and you haven't even come into contact with them yet. Here are some signs that you've got a Negative Nancy/Nigel in your circle:

Pessimistic: Life can be tough, and sometimes we'll go through things that bring us down. But as the saying goes, "After the rain comes the sun," and those frowns eventually turn into smiles. But with negative people, those frowns are permanent. They never have anything good to say, and will put their negative spin on everything. If you tell them good news, they'll congratulate you, but still have something bad to say about it. Even when something good happens to them, they will have something bad to say about it. For example, your friend just bought a new car—but all they can do is complain about how much the car note costs every month.

Don't Feel Hopeful About the Future: Negative people don't feel excited about the future because they're always worrying about what could go wrong. No matter what goals they're working on, they can only see doom and gloom for the future. Nor are they hopeful about anyone else's future. When a friend in the group gets married, the Negative Nancy/Nigel's response is, "I don't know why they bothered—haven't they heard the statistics about marriage? Over fifty percent of them end in divorce, and the other fifty percent are probably hanging on for dear life."

Ignore Solutions and Focus on Problems: Is your friend or partner the type who refuses to acknowledge the solutions? No matter how viable the solution may sound, they'll find something that won't work. As a result, they wallow in self-pity and never take action to get themselves out of their situation. For example, let's say your friend has just lost her job, but she makes awesome cookies, so you suggest she bake some cookies and set up a stall on a busy street. She comes up with twenty-five reasons why it won't work—but when she gets kicked out of her apartment because she can't afford to pay the rent, the first person she asks for a loan is you!

Reject Compliments: You can never compliment a Negative Nancy/Nigel, because they won't accept it. Negative people are extremely insecure and don't think very highly of themselves. They wear their insecurities on their sleeves, and for every compliment, they've got something bad to say about themselves. If you say, "Your hair looks amazing," they'll respond, "But it shows too much of my big forehead." If you say, "You look good in those jeans," they'll say, "They make my legs look fat." It's a pointless endeavor trying to compliment a negative person.

Are Judgmental: Negative people have such high standards for themselves and others that they are constantly pointing out other people's flaws. No one can do anything right, no one ever looks good enough, and they're always gossiping. You don't need to read the gossip magazines when a negative person is around; they've got all the tea and take great pride in spilling it.

Focus on the Past: There are some things in life you can't change, and there's no point in dwelling on them. But a negative person can't help themselves; they spend night and day agonizing over what went wrong, what they could have done better, and how much they wish they could turn back the hands of time. While it's true you should acknowledge your past so you don't repeat it in the future, you can't stay there. It's like driving a car and always looking in the rearview mirror—eventually, you'll crash. Metaphorically speaking, the rearview mirror is small for a reason: you're only meant to glance at your past every so often, because what you *should* be focusing on is the bright future you've got ahead of you. One of the main reasons negative people dwell on the past is that, as mentioned, they don't have any hope for the future.

Don't Challenge Themselves: Negative people stay in their comfort zones because they don't like challenging themselves. They don't see the point because they've convinced themselves they're incapable. When you suggest trying something new, they've always got an excuse as to why it's not a good idea. But what they fail to understand is that the person who doesn't challenge themselves never grows and will never know what they are truly capable of.

Too Sensitive: You can't crack a joke around a negative person because they'll take it to heart and get upset about it. When someone is always focused on the negative, they have an unstable state of mind. It doesn't even need to be a joke; a random conversation that they've taken personally can lead to them having a hissy fit. Negative people end up ruining relationships because they're too sensitive. Everyone has to walk on eggshells around them, which makes it no fun to associate with them.

Constantly Worried: Negative people worry a lot because they're always expecting the worst to happen. When they think about the future, they don't imagine all the amazing things that might happen; they focus on all the things that could go wrong. The acronym for fear is *False Evidence Appearing Real*. In other words, the negative person spends so much time thinking the worst, they convince themselves it's real and it's going to happen. This creates a feeling of depression and they can't think about anything else other than how awful life is.

THE ENERGY VAMPIRE

All empaths are familiar with energy vampires, and have most likely had an experience with several throughout their life. Whether intentionally or unintentionally, energy vampires leach off your emotional energy and leave you feeling completely exhausted after spending time with them. An energy vampire can be anyone—a friend, family member, work colleague or neighbor. Just know that once they lock into you, it's very difficult to get rid of them. The key to protecting yourself from an energy vampire is either to not give them access to your life from the get-go, or to keep them at arm's length. Before I go into the signs that someone is an energy vampire, you also need to know that there are six different types:

1. **The Dominator:** A lot of alpha personalities are dominator vampires. On the surface, it appears that they're just assertive go-getters who know what they want out of life. But that's not the case —they have deep-seated insecurities and fear being wrong or weak. To avoid this, they use intimidation. They also have the tendency to be very loud and overbearing, with rigid beliefs. They see the world through a black-and-white lens; there are no gray areas. Dominator vampires are often bigoted, homophobic, sexist, or racist.

2. **The Narcissist:** Narcissist vampires are terribly selfish and are only interested in what they can get out of people. They seek out empaths because they are an easy source of supply. Narcissistic supply is basically like heroin to an addict. They need it—and if they don't get it, they suffer from withdrawals. Narcissistic supply is the constant supply of admiration and attention they need to survive. Narcissists come across as being the most confident people in the world, but they're extremely insecure. To make themselves feel better, they create a false narrative about themselves that paints them as a picture of perfection. They then seek out individuals who will cater to this narrative by praising and admiring them. The narcissist energy vampire has no interest in your life; all they're concerned about is their narcissistic supply.

3. **The Judgmental:** Judgmental vampires hate themselves and so make themselves feel better by projecting their self-hatred onto others. The terrible way they treat people is a reflection of how they feel about themselves. To bolster their egos, they prey on people's insecurities to make them feel ashamed, small, or pathetic.

4. **The Melodramatic:** Melodramatic vampires are addicted to negative emotions and therefore seek out constant drama. They either cause the problems, or they look for problems to get involved with because it creates a false sense of security. They surround themselves with drama so they don't have to face the reality of their fragmented lives. Like most energy vampires, they're extremely insecure, and when they're consumed with drama and the attention that comes with it, they feel special and important.

5. **The Innocent:** With some energy vampires, there is no malicious intent; they are just codependent. They are not good at helping themselves, and because you're so giving, they rely on you for everything. They will say things like, "I don't know what I'd do without you." And they genuinely mean it—you're their biggest support, and no matter how you're feeling, you always make time for them. They take so much of your time and energy that you have nothing left to give yourself.

6. **The Martyr or Victim:** These energy vampires get what they want by making people feel guilty. They believe that all their suffering is because of what other people have done to them. They refuse to accept that their own bad decisions and actions are the reason for their abysmal state. They suf-

fer from terribly low self-esteem, often as a result of not receiving the love and attention they needed during childhood. They feel unaccepted and unlovable, and to deal with it, they make you feel guilty to gain sympathy. You'll know when you're in the presence of a martyr/victim vampire because they're always throwing pity parties. For example, they'll talk about what an awful day they've had because of their boss. Or they'll start crying for no reason, and when you ask them what's wrong, they'll bang on about how unfair life is for them.

Despite the different types, all energy vampires are essentially the same, and their main aim is to drain people of their energy. Here are the typical signs of an energy vampire:

They Bully or Criticize: As mentioned, all energy vampires are insecure—and they want everyone around them to feel the same. If they can keep their victims feeling just as insecure as them, the energy vampire will keep getting the attention they crave. For example:

- "I *told* you this project would be too hard for you, but you went ahead and took it on anyway. *Now* look at the mess you've gotten yourself into!" (You've made a couple of typos and they're acting like it's the end of the world.)

- "Why do you always put so much salt in the food? You know I've got high blood pressure." (You literally added one pinch of salt!)

They're Codependent: In a codependent relationship, one person is the taker, the other is the giver. The energy vampire is always the taker, and the empath is the giver. The giver takes on the responsibility for meeting the needs of the taker, and if those needs are not met, it causes problems in the relationship. For example:

- You forgot to call your friend before his football match and give him a pep talk. His team lost the match, and so he blames you because you forgot to call.

- You had other plans, so you were unable to drive your boyfriend across town to meet his friend. He asked you at the last minute and so it was impossible to cancel. Apparently, because you didn't drop your plans for him, and he couldn't make it, his friendships are now strained.

They Use Ultimatums or Guilt Trips: Energy vampires know shame is a powerful weapon against caring and compassionate people, so they will make their victims feel guilty to get what they want. Additionally, they believe ultimatums are a great way to get someone's attention and entice them to do something they don't want to do. For example:

- "If you truly love me, you'll call him right now and say you can no longer speak to him. If you don't, this relationship's over."

- "You can't leave me—I'll die without you in my life."

They Have a Victim Mentality: Energy vampires don't take responsibility for their actions and blame other people for their circumstances. They're looking for emotional support to make themselves feel better. For example:

- "Nothing I do is ever good enough for my boss. I try my hardest at work, and he won't give me a break." (Your friend is always late for work and does the bare minimum, but still expects a paycheck at the end of the month.)

- "If only my mom had been there for me when I was younger, I would be in a much better place right now."

They Take the Limelight: When you're upset or sad, your energy reserves are depleted, and because energy vampires are dependent upon your emotional energy, they will shift the conversation so you are focusing on them instead of yourself. For example:

- "I know you don't get paid that much, but at least you enjoy your job—I hate my job. Please help me find a new one."

- "I understand that you're really stressed out at work, but I need to talk to you right now about all the hell I'm going through with David."

They've Got to Be Better Than You: Energy vampires have narcissistic tendencies and can't handle it when the spotlight is not on them. They find it difficult to be happy about other people's success and deal with their jealousy by sucking on their victim's energy. For example:

- "Nice to hear you got a new job, but I just applied for a job today that pays twice as much as that and I really need it. Can you help me make sure my résumé is on point to ensure I get the job?"

- "Congratulations on passing the test. How many certifications do you need now before you're on my level?"

They're Surrounded by Drama: There's always some type of drama going on in the energy vampire's life. They are surrounded by chaos and ensure that they drag their victims into every last bit of it.

- "I need you to come with me to the store. I bought a jacket yesterday and it's got a hole in it already. I want my money back." (You go with her to the store, and instead of politely asking for a refund, she starts raising hell.)

- "I got sacked from my job today. I need you to go back there with me so I can collect my last paycheck." (You go with her, and she starts cussing out her manager and the other employees she doesn't like.)

They Lack Personal Accountability: Another narcissistic characteristic energy vampires have is their charismatic nature. They tend to get away with a lot because they come across as so charming. They are very sly, and when they've done something wrong, they'll shove the blame onto someone else without a second thought. That person is often you.

- "I just spent $100 on my mom's credit card. I'm going to tell her you needed to use it urgently. I'll pay it back, but if she asks, can you cover for me please?"

- "Why is it that I never get promoted at work and people who haven't been here as long as me get promoted?" (Because they do what needs to be done to get promoted; the energy vampire doesn't.)

The Drama Queen

Despite the name, a drama queen can be a man or a woman. A drama queen is someone who goes over the top about everything. They are very dramatic and intense and crave attention. They always need you to help them out with one problem or another. At first, you don't mind helping out—until there's another issue immediately after. It doesn't take long for you to realize that *they're* the problem. Their problems are always a matter of urgency, and they use them to control you. Eventually, your life ends up revolving around their constant dramas. Here are the main signs of a drama queen:

Conveniently Ill: This is especially true when a drama queen is in a relationship. They will miraculously fall ill when you're about to go out with friends, or when you're spending time alone. Since you're excited about going out, they'll do everything they can to make you feel guilty for not dropping your plans and giving them the attention they deserve because of this mystery illness.

The Queen Has Arrived: The drama queen takes great pleasure in making the most dramatic and grand entrances. They will turn up to events late and make as much noise as possible when they enter the building to ensure they are the center of attention.

Ongoing Conflicts: When they do get into it with someone, they ensure the conflict is an ongoing one because it gives them an emotional high. Even when the person involved apologizes because they don't want it to continue, the drama queen refuses to accept the apology, preferring to keep the conflict going.

Starts Conflict: Because drama queens like to be on an emotional high all the time, they'll stir up trouble intentionally to get everyone into a reactive state. They'll do things like tell a work colleague they overheard the manager talking badly about them. The hope is that they'll confront the manager so it turns into a work-related brawl they can enjoy watching for a while.

Extreme Emotional Reactions: It doesn't matter what it is; the drama queen has an extreme emotional reaction to everything. You can't have a normal conversation with them because they'll scream and holler at everything.

Very Pessimistic: Drama queens are very irrational and think the worst about everything. They don't think anything through and just jump to conclusions whenever something doesn't work out as planned. For example, if you've got to cancel plans because of a work deadline, they'll assume you don't care about them. If you can't drive them where they need to go because you've got to take your mother to a doctor's appointment, they'll assume you're just making excuses because you don't want to spend time with them during the drive.

They Throw Tantrums: Drama queens act like two-year-olds, and they'll throw the biggest tantrums when they don't get their way. They don't care where they are at the time. It could be at a family gathering, a work function, or out in public. They believe the world revolves around them, and they'll do whatever is necessary to make sure it does. For the drama queen, it's all about being the center of attention, and they don't care how bad it makes them or the people they're with look.

Center of Attention: As mentioned, drama queens love to be the center of attention. They don't do two-way conversations because everything is about *them*. Whenever they get a new item of clothing, or get their hair done, they've got to make a big spectacle of it. If they notice the crowd is gravitating towards someone else, they'll do something ridiculous like collapse on the floor to make sure all eyes are on them.

How to Deal With Toxic People

Regardless of the type of dark empath that shows up in your life, they are all toxic. The good news is you can learn to manage them in a way that doesn't disrupt your life. Here are some tips:

Don't Take It Personally: At some point, you'll wonder why you keep attracting toxic people and assume there's something wrong with you. It's important to remember that there's absolutely nothing wrong with you, and you should not take it personally. This is especially true when it comes to the manipulators and malignant narcissists, who will falsely accuse you or misconstrue everything you say. Their behavior is not *your* problem—it's *theirs*. When you find yourself in an uncomfortable situation, don't react, but mindfully acknowledge what's been said and let it go. Don't try and evaluate or understand—just let their words float by.

Set Boundaries: Toxic people don't like boundaries because they believe they can invade your space whenever they like. But if you're going to get any rest from toxic people, you'll need to put your foot down and set some boundaries. Setting boundaries prevents resentment, frustration, and all the other negative emotions that come with dealing with toxic people. Boundaries teach people how to treat you, and place limitations around your emotions, mental health, time, and body. These invisible borders protect you from being manipulated, drained, and used by toxic people.

Personal boundaries help you to live a balanced and fulfilled life. When you give everyone and everything unlimited access to you, you can get lost in your relationships, service to others, work, and family obligations. People who create boundaries around their lives are respected by others because it is clear that you put yourself first. They free you from being dictated to by others so you can live your life the way you desire. People with strong boundaries have higher self-esteem and less stress because their well-being is the most important thing to them. Here are five steps to setting boundaries:

1. **Establish Your Boundaries:** Write your boundaries down so you're clear about them. Boundaries are not about anyone else but you; therefore, think about what you need to make you happy. Ask yourself the following questions:

    - What things or people cause me unnecessary discomfort or stress?
    - What things do I not look forward to throughout the day?
    - Who in my life drains my energy?
    - When do I feel the most exhausted?
    - When do I feel valued, supported, and safe?

    Now get a piece of paper and draw a circle that takes up half the page. In the middle of the circle, write down everything that makes you feel stress-free and safe such as:
    - Saying "no" to draining people
    - Leaving work problems at work
    - A consistent daily routine
    - Kind words from your partner
    - Open and clear communication from friends and family

Outside the circle, write down all the things that cause you emotional exhaustion, annoyance, pain, and discomfort. These are the toxic people and situations stressing you out. For example:

- Your parents trying to run your life
- Taking work home and working until all hours of the night
- Worrying about what people think about you
- Your roommate eating your food and not replacing it
- Your partner's controlling behavior
- People asking you uncomfortable questions

Now you have clarified the good and bad people and situations in your life, it's time to communicate your boundaries.

2. **Communicate Your Boundaries**

   Communicating your boundaries will be uncomfortable because your toxic friends and family members are so used to having access to you whenever they want. Nevertheless, take a deep breath and express your boundaries in an assertive, direct, and kind way. Here are some examples:

   - **Social Media:** "Please ask before you post anything about me on social media."
   - **Your Possessions:** "Please ask before you borrow anything that belongs to me."
   - **Mental Health:** "I respect your opinion, so please respect mine. I do not appreciate you forcing me to see things from your point of view."
   - **Comments:** "What you just said was offensive, and I don't appreciate it."

- **Conversations:** "This is not something I want to talk about right now."

- **Personal Space:** "I don't feel comfortable when you impose on my personal space like that."

- **Emotional Dumping:** "I'm sorry you're going through this, but now is not the time to discuss it with me—I don't have the capacity to deal with it at the moment."

- **Energy:** "Sorry, that is not something I can participate in right now."

- **Time:** "Please let me know in advance if you're going to be late." Or, "I've only got an hour to spare."

As you will have noticed, setting boundaries isn't about calling all the toxic people in your phone book and letting them know what you expect. Wait for the situation to arise, and then say what you need to say. As mentioned, it will take some grit—and not just because you don't like conflict, but because the people you're enforcing the boundaries upon are not used to you being so assertive. They may mock you, or laugh, but stand your ground.

Tip: Don't compromise with your boundaries. Some people will try and get you to break your rules for them. Don't tolerate it. The minute you start making allowances for someone, they will keep pushing until your boundaries have completely disappeared. For example, you may have a work colleague whom you've told not to call you after work hours. One day, she calls and says, "I know you told me not to call you after work hours, but I've got an emergency." When you agree to speak to her, first of all, I can guarantee it won't be an emergency. Second, she will keep calling you after work hours anytime she has an emergency. In a situation like this, after the third warning, stop answering the phone.

3. **Start Saying "No"**

As far as I'm concerned, "no" is the most liberating word on the planet. It will set you free from tying yourself up in so many unnecessary engagements. Do you agree to things often, only to regret it once you've sat down and thought about it? It's better to say you'll get back to them after you've had time to go over your schedule instead of saying yes immediately. In this day and age, it's not uncommon for people to feel guilty for saying "no" because it comes across as being unkind. But in reality, the person who says "no" all the time has more to offer than the person who says "yes" all the time. A person who says "yes" all the time never shows up as the best version of themselves; because they've given so much of themselves away, they have no time for self-care. Meanwhile, the person who says "no" all the time invests in themselves often because they've got the time to do so. If you're not sure how to say "no," here are some tips:

Practice Saying No: When someone asks you face to face to do something outside your capacity, you've got to be prepared to say "no." You won't always have the luxury of saying "no" through an email or text message when it's most convenient for you. The best way to get around this is to practice saying "no" and have your excuses ready. Here are a few suggestions:

- "I would love to go, and I appreciate the invite, but I'll have to give it a miss because I'm trying to focus on some other stuff at the moment."

- "I've got so much on right now, I just don't have the time to help. So, sorry, I won't be able to. I hope you get it done."

- "I can't make it I'm afraid; I've committed to going to the gym every night until I reach my ideal body type."

Practice saying these in front of a mirror until they become natural to you.

Don't Explain Yourself: Even when you give an excuse, some people are determined to get you to comply; for example:

- You say you can't go out for a drink because you've got other plans. They will then ask what day you're free.

- You say you can't make it because you don't have a babysitter. They tell you to bring the kids with you.

- You say you can't help someone out because you've got a deadline to meet. They say they don't mind waiting until you've finished your project.

When you run into a situation like this, simply thank them for asking/inviting you, but tell them you won't be able to make it—and leave it at that.

Say Later: As mentioned, instead of saying "no," say "later." Say this to everyone who asks you. Here are some tips on how to say "later":

- "Thanks for asking. Let me check whether it's my turn to pick the kids up from school and I'll get back to you."

- "That sounds great! But I'll need to think about it. I'll get back to you in a couple of days."

- "Thanks for the invite, but I'll need to ask my partner if we've got anything going on that night."

- I'll need to check my diary. I'll get back to you shortly."

If it's a work colleague, ask them to email or text their request so you don't forget. This will make it easier for you to decline when you do eventually get back to them.

Use Your Body Language: To really drive home the message, use your body language to say no. After all, according to experts, the majority of our communication is nonverbal. Here are some body language tips that scream "NO!":

- Point your toes in the opposite direction to the person asking you. Our feet always point in the direction we want to go, and in your case, it's far away from the toxic individual in front of you!

- To let the person know you don't wish to discuss it any further, cross your arms across your chest. The chest is the largest part of the body, and what you indirectly say when you cross your arms is, "I'm guarded, and I don't want you anywhere near me."

- Turn your upper body away so you're not facing them. Just imagine a person with bad hygiene hugging you. You automatically turn your body away to protect yourself from being assaulted by the smell.

Practice Self-Care: We live in such a fast-paced world that most people don't have the time to practice self-care. But research suggests that it helps prevent burnout, makes us more stable, emotionally intelligent, creative and confident. Each week, set aside two hours of uninterrupted time to do something relaxing. That might include going for a massage, a facial, going to the beach, or going shopping. Whatever makes you happy, do it. During this time, let everyone know you won't be available. In fact, to prevent any boundary violations, just turn your phone off. In case you are wondering what self-care has to do with setting boundaries, the answer is that it gives you time to reflect and think about your life so you can structure it in a way that's best for you. It gives you clarity of mind and strengthens your mental capacity so you are better able to enforce your boundaries. Additionally, self-care enables you to show up as the best version of yourself so you can be a brighter light to the world.

Enforce the Consequences: Since your toxic friends and family members are not used to you being so forthright, it will take some time for them to get used to your boundaries. You'll also need to remind yourself that some toxic people refuse to respect boundaries—which is when you'll have to get ruthless and cut them off. (I'll discuss that later.) When it comes to enforcing the consequences, use the "three strikes and you're out" rule. After the first violation, say, "I think I told you last time not to do that. Please respect my boundaries." If it happens again, say, "Like I told you last time, please respect my boundaries—and if it happens again, I won't be communicating with you." If it happens again, don't waste any time—block that person on all platforms. If it's a work colleague, let them know that you don't wish to engage with them unless it's work-related.

Don't Give Them Access: As mentioned, toxic people know exactly who they can manipulate because everything they do is calculated down to the letter. But they also don't like wasting time.

Take narcissists, for example. Their main concern is getting supply; it's like a drug to them, and if they can't get it when they want it, they'll move on to the next person. In general, when toxic people realize their plans are not working because they can't get access to you, they give up. When they call or want to engage at work, you can say something like:

- "Sorry, I can't talk now; I need to get this project done."

- "I need to get ready for a meeting tomorrow; I can't chat now."

The toxic person will probably let it slide the first or second time, but when you keep giving them excuses as to why you can't hang out, you'll probably get some pushback in the form of passive-aggressive behavior. Ignore it and let them sulk.

Give Them a Time Limit: There will be times when you can't escape from toxic people. In such instances, give them a time limit. If you bump into them at a dinner party, let them talk for five minutes and move on to the next person. Unfortunately, some of the toxic people in your life will be family members, which means you can't avoid them during the holidays and other celebrations. Again, limit the time you spend with them by mingling with other people. When it comes to toxic people calling you, let them know you don't have much time to chat because you've got errands to run. It may seem exhausting making all these excuses, but it's ten times more exhausting having to spend time with these people.

Switch It Up: Does a work colleague or a family member always catch you when you're trying to get stuff done? Maybe you can never have lunch in peace because the person who sits opposite you at work always wants to complain about management. Or you can't escape from your trifling cousin because she gets on the same bus as you every morning. Switch it up and start doing things differently. Take a walk for lunch and eat your sandwiches on a park bench. To avoid your cousin, start getting an earlier bus. If the toxic people in your life can't find you, they can't bother you.

Encourage Them to See a Therapist: Toxic people don't take too kindly to being told there's something wrong with them and they need help. However, hurt people hurt people, and toxic people were not born that way. Their life experiences have caused them to have a chip on their shoulder, and if they don't get help, they'll carry their bitterness to the grave. Sit your friend or family member down and kindly point out some of their behaviors that you find worrying. Explain that they may need to see someone about it. They will either agree and start looking for a therapist, or they'll disagree and cause an argument. Just remember that their anger is not directed at you.

Keep It to Yourself: Toxic people will often use what you say against you. Or they'll gossip with other friends about what you've said. Avoid this by keeping your personal information to yourself. When it comes to your interactions with toxic people, be as tight-lipped as possible. They'll attempt to pry and get more out of you, but maintain your composure and don't give in. Let's say you're having a conversation at work and they get really pushy. Say something like, "I'm sorry, but I'd rather not share such things about my private life at work." A statement like this will quickly shut the conversation down.

Be Calm: The mere thought of having interactions with a toxic person can cause anxiety and make your heart beat faster than normal. However, it's important to stay calm or you'll work yourself into a frenzy. When anxiety strikes during an interaction with someone, ground yourself by doing the following:

- Breathe deeply and slowly.

- Don't tense your muscles; relax them instead.

- Let their words float by, and repeat a calming mantra to yourself.

- If you can, distract yourself by closing your eyes and visualizing something peaceful, or find something else to focus on other than the conversation.

See a Therapist: As mentioned, there are some toxic people like family members whom you can't escape from. No matter how many avoidance tactics you use, you've still got to interact with them—which can have a negative effect on your mental health. If you're finding it difficult to cope with a situation like this, get some professional help. A therapist will be able to assist you in dealing with your unique circumstances and put an action plan together that will work for you.

If you're in a relationship with a dark empath, or you suspect a friend or a family member is a dark empath and you want to help them, your first step is to understand why they are the way they are. I don't believe people are inherently evil; whatever's wrong with them in their adult years is due to childhood trauma. As with most empaths, their gift was stunted during childhood because their parents didn't understand it. The only difference between the empath and the dark empath is their trauma has manifested as darkness. So to get started, let's take a look at dark empaths and inner child trauma.

PLEASE NOTE: If your partner/friend/loved one is not ready to change, don't force it on them. Learn everything you can about dark empaths, and when they're ready to start their healing journey, you can support them.

CHAPTER 3:

DARK EMPATHS AND INNER CHILD TRAUMA

Whether we've acknowledged it or not, we all have an inner child. We refer to it by saying things like, "That's the kid in me," or, "I've got the faith of a child." However, most people are unaware of how much their inner child influences their present life. The inner child is a psychological concept that was first discussed by psychologist Carl Jung. He believed that the inner child represented everything fun, free, and exciting—because, in general, that's how children are: they love life, and they're always looking forward to tomorrow. Other experts during the same era referred to the inner child as the adult expression of childhood. But psychologist Dr. Diana Raab highlighted two aspects of the inner child: the healthy inner child, and the traumatized inner child. The healthy inner child is the one raised by well-rounded parents who were able to give their children the tools they needed to become fully functioning members of society both physically and emotionally. On the other hand, the traumatized inner child was raised by parents who lacked the ability to raise their children effectively, and, in some cases, were abusive.

Childhood trauma causes severe psychological damage and stunts emotional growth, making it difficult to live a fulfilling life. One of the reasons empaths become dark empaths is childhood trauma. The issues they have are subconsciously led by their traumatized inner child. The wounds they endured during childhood were never healed. They developed coping mechanisms to deal with the trauma, and they're still affected by it now. Here are some of the wounds that may have been inflicted during childhood:

THE ABANDONMENT WOUND

Most parents are not aware that their children are empaths and will unintentionally neglect them. Empath children are often told to stop being silly, or punished for being too sensitive. This leaves the child feeling as if they've been physically, mentally, and emotionally abandoned. Empath children have a deep desire to feel a connection to their parents. Since they can tune into others' emotions, empath children always want to make sure their parents and siblings are okay. But it is not uncommon for this desire not to be reciprocated. When parents don't show up for their children like they need them to, the children feel abandoned and start asking themselves questions such as, "Am I not good enough?" "What's wrong with me?" or, "Why don't my parents love me the way I love them?" They deal with these feelings of rejection by developing coping mechanisms such as:

- Building a wall around themselves and becoming extremely independent so they don't need anyone.

- Not developing meaningful relationships, and when someone does start getting too close, they sabotage it so they can't abandon them.

- They become codependent or a people pleaser to avoid causing problems and make everyone happy so they don't leave them.

- They neglect themselves because abandonment has taught them that they are not a priority and that everyone else comes first.

Dark empaths with abandonment issues are either fiercely independent and never reach out to anyone for help no matter how badly they're suffering, or they focus so much on others that they completely neglect themselves. Either way, abandonment causes them to have unbalanced relationships because they're either too tuned in, or they're detached.

THE TRUST WOUND

The trust wound causes a feeling of betrayal. It happens when a parent fails to fulfill a promise, or they unintentionally fail to take care of an emotional need. The latter is most common because, as mentioned, the parents of empath children are often unaware of their child's gift and will therefore invalidate their feelings. When children stop trusting the people assigned to care for them, that lack of trust is internalized and they stop trusting *themselves*. An empath's instincts tell them whom they should and should not trust. So, when they are betrayed by the people they trust, they start doubting their ability to rely on their gut instincts—since they were unable to sense that they couldn't trust their own parents. Some of the coping mechanisms they may have developed as a child include:

- Refusing to trust anyone (including themselves) until they've proved themselves to them.

- Attracting people who will betray them, or betraying people before they betray them.

- Low self-esteem and self-doubt because they don't trust themselves.

- Difficulty forming close relationships, to protect themselves from getting hurt.

- Becoming extremely controlling so they don't get hurt.

- The need for constant validation because they don't feel worthy.

Dark empaths with the trust wound often become stagnant in life because they put too much time and energy into the wrong things. They question everything and everyone, including themselves, and become completely obsessed with whom they can and cannot trust.

THE NEGLECT WOUND

When parents fail to prioritize the needs of their children, it causes them to feel neglected. These could be emotional needs such as helping them understand and connect with their feelings, comforting them when they are in distress, or listening to them when they need to express themselves. Parents can also neglect their children's physical needs, such as through failure to provide adequate safety, clothing, and food. When children are raised in environments like this, they learn that they are irrelevant, their needs don't deserve recognition, and other people are more important. They can also develop the belief that they don't need new things and that, unless something is totally destroyed, they should keep using it. They are made to feel as if the bare minimum is enough, and they don't deserve anything more than that. Some of the coping mechanisms they may have developed include:

- Living with a scarcity mentality and settling for scraps and leftovers.

- Denying their body of its normal care and comfort.

- Making other people a priority while neglecting themselves.

- Being afraid of having needs.

- Feeling vulnerable or weak because they have needs.

- A sense of guilt or unworthiness when they ask for help or support.

- Frustration or anger because their needs are constantly rejected.

- Disconnecting from their inner guidance or intuition because they don't feel worthy of it.

THE GUILT WOUND

Those affected by the guilt wound are raised in toxic, abusive, and neglectful environments. Their parents made them feel guilty for having needs and for any behavior they deemed unacceptable. Instead of walking the child through their emotions and helping them understand them, they shame the child for having them. The child can never be their authentic self because they are made to feel like a burden. Additionally, people are afflicted by the guilt wound when parents make their children feel guilty for their life's troubles. They will say things like, "If I hadn't given birth to you, I wouldn't have these problems," or, "Life has been nothing but difficult since you were born." Empaths go out of their way not to hurt anyone, so when parents treat an empath child as if they are the problem, they internalize these beliefs. The false beliefs eat away at the child's self-esteem, confidence, and self-worth. The parents no longer need to blame the children for anything because as soon as something goes wrong, they blame themselves. In adulthood, the guilt wound causes a person to avoid pain by becoming a "people pleaser," or a "fixer." Coping mechanisms include:

- Feeling guilty for having needs and acting out on those needs.

- Feeling shame because of who they are.

- Feeling like they don't deserve the good things in life. They believe they are not worthy of being taken care of, being loved, or living an abundant life.

- Attracting narcissists and manipulative people who make them feel guilty for being who they are.

- Projecting their pain by manipulating and guilt-tripping others.

- Allowing people to take advantage of their energy, time, love and resources.

- Having poor emotional and energetic boundaries because they feel it's their fault that other people are suffering, and that they're responsible for others' emotions.

They've been carrying the guilt, shame and pain of everyone around them since they were a child and it's become the norm to them.

Since they've carried the burdens of others for so long, they have become immune to how heavy a weight it is and how much it's holding them back in life. Other people's trauma becomes so intertwined with theirs that they don't know which emotions belong to others and which belong to them.

How a Person's Unhealed Wounds Become Their Guide

It's important to understand that, no matter how abusive a person's parents were, they didn't hurt them intentionally. Parents can only give their children what they received from their parents, and most of the time, that wasn't much. You see, there is no manual on parenting, and the problem is that, to be a good parent, you need to be a well-balanced and emotionally mature person. Unfortunately, these are not lessons taught in school; therefore, the average person is not well-balanced or emotionally mature. Most people don't think about things such as emotional stability and psychological well-being until a life-changing event occurs. A lot of parents are unaware that the way they treat their children—whether good or bad—has long-lasting psychological effects. Something as seemingly trivial as ignoring, dismissing, or rejecting a child can cause them to suffer from abandonment issues during adulthood. Some of you may have gone through more traumatic experiences such as physical, sexual, or emotional abuse. Abused children typically go into survival mode; they can't escape, so they do what's necessary to stay alive, and that may involve burying the trauma. Because you didn't deal with it at the time, it is still a very prominent part of you, and these unhealed wounds become your guide in life.

Nevertheless, we are all unique individuals, and trauma affects each one of us differently. You may have endured some terrible things as a child, but today, you're living your best life, as if you had the most glorious upbringing. But there are some who don't have this privilege; their lives are driven by their unresolved trauma, and it manifests in the most horrific ways. Our emotions speak to us from the inside; they let us know when there's a problem. However, to avoid confronting the pain, we ignore these emotions by doing what we've always done: burying them and getting on with life. For these people, pain becomes the norm, and they live as "walking wounded." To overcome these inner child wounds, healing is essential. You'll learn all about inner child healing in Chapter 4.

CHAPTER 4:

INNER CHILD HEALING

Before we get started, I'd like you to know that inner child healing is a difficult and emotional journey. There is absolutely no pressure or rush to start this process now. If your partner/friend/loved one doesn't feel ready, they can skip this chapter and move on to the next. Because I can tell you from experience that it is brutal, and you won't realize how intense it is until you get started. But if they're ready to begin their healing journey, I want them to know the following:

- You are innocent. The pain that was inflicted upon you is not a reflection of who you are. You did nothing to deserve it.

- You were just a child and you did everything right. Your abusers were adults, and they did everything wrong.

- What happened to you does not determine who you are.

- Complete healing is available to you.

You may have been so hurt as a child that you believe you're damaged beyond repair—but you're not. There is a part of you that still has hope, or you wouldn't be reading this book. You're here because you want to heal and get better, and the part of you that still has hope is the part that's going to get you through this.

Before we get started, let me give you some advice about what to expect when you start healing. Apart from the obvious life changes of feeling happier, having a more positive outlook on life, and feeling less overwhelmed, your social circle will change. When I started my healing journey, I had a lot of toxic people in my life (the type you read about in Chapter 2), and I'm assuming you've got similar people in *your* life at the moment too. To begin with, these people will encourage you to remain where you are. When you tell them what you're doing, they'll say things like, "There's nothing wrong with you. You're perfect the way you are. We love this version of you." Not because they're intentionally trying to hold you back, but because the unhealed part of them needs *you* to stay unhealed because otherwise they will no longer be able to ma-nipulate you, take advantage of you, or relate to you. As the saying goes, "Like attracts like," and it was your pain that connected you with them in the first place. Because you're an empath, it will be difficult to ignore your loved ones. You love them and want to make them happy—and up until this point, your relationship has been all about prioritizing their needs over yours. But you can't afford to do that anymore. In order to become the person you were destined to be, healing is essential. When you don't give in to their demands, you'll start losing these people as friends. Your energies will be so misaligned that you won't need to leave them—they'll leave you. As the saying goes, "Misery loves company."

HOW TO CONNECT WITH YOUR INNER CHILD

Before you can heal your inner child, you've got to connect with it, and you can achieve this through meditation. It gives you the opportunity to reach out to that little girl or boy and meet them in their moment of need. You can return to the time when you were in pain and at your most vulnerable but there was no one there to comfort you and tell you everything was going to be all right. You can tell yourself everything you needed to hear and give yourself the unconditional love you deserved as a child. To truly benefit from this meditation, make it a part of your daily routine. The more you visit your inner child, the better you will get to know them.

Inner Child Meditation

- Go somewhere quiet and peaceful where you won't be interrupted.

- Get into a comfortable seated position. Focus your mind and relax your body.

- Breathe in slowly and deeply; breathe out slowly and deeply.

- The more you breathe, the more relaxed you will feel.

- Stop deep-breathing and start breathing at a normal rhythm for a few seconds.

- You will feel your eyes become heavy.

- Relax your jaw and your cheeks.

- Relax your arms, shoulders and hands.

- Release the tension in your stomach.

- Your legs and feet will feel heavy as the relaxation deepens.

- Relaxation will also make you feel warm.

- Visualize yourself as a child (it would help to look at some childhood photos before getting started).

- Focus on yourself as a child and take note of what you look like. What color is your hair? How is it styled? What are you wearing? Are you sitting or standing?

- Keep the image in your mind and focus on your inner child.

- Is the child making any noise? How is he/she behaving?

- Stop focusing on your inner child and breathe at a normal rhythm for a few seconds.

- Visualize a dark, smoky, scary-looking bubble. It's big enough for your inner child to fit inside, and it's positioned next to your inner child.

- Focus on the bubble and what's inside it.

- You might see the distressing situations you experienced as a child, or the heavy negative emotions you felt because of what you were forced to endure.

- When you were a child, you coped by creating stories about these distressing situations and the negative emotions you felt. Maybe your story was about how terrible you were, that you suffered because there was something wrong with you, and that you deserved everything you got.

- These stories play on repeat in your subconscious mind and they've caused you to become stagnant in life. The universe wants to give you so much, but there is a blockage because of your unresolved trauma.

- Inhale slowly and deeply.

- Exhale slowly and deeply and free yourself of the pain attached to those stories.

- Stretch your arms out towards your inner child and give him/her a big hug.

- While you're holding your inner child, give them all the unconditional love you wanted as a child.

- While you're hugging your inner child, the dark, smoky bubble starts to disintegrate; all the negativity is fading away because of all the love you're giving to your inner child.

- Start breathing at a normal pace.

- Let go of your inner child, move away and look at him/her.

- The bubble has reappeared, but it is brilliantly see-through and filled with love, creativity and dreams.

- There were a few happy memories during your childhood and you can see them in the bubble.

- The only thing you can see in the bubble is positive emotions.

- Focus on the bubble and take in the amazing energy it is radiating.

- You own this state, and you can access it anytime you want.

- Smile as you accept that this is now your reality.

- Focus on your inner child. Notice that they are now beaming and glowing with joy; his/her soul is no longer in distress.

- Your inner child loved doing things that children enjoy such as skipping, playing games, jumping and running. You can remember this now.

- Your inner child is happy that you came to rescue them and they can't wait to have more positive experiences with you to store in the bubble.

- Stretch out your arms and hug your inner child tightly.

- Your inner child is overflowing with love and you can feel it becoming a part of you.

- You have become one with your inner child.

- Let go of your inner child, start breathing at a normal pace, and focus on your breath.

- Your body now radiates with peace.

- You have connected with your inner child and taught him/her that they are wonderful and deserving of all the love life has to offer.

You are amazing, and I'm truly proud of you. I know from experience that this is not easy, but you've overcome the first hurdle. I felt awesome after I had completed this meditation, like I was finally free— but it gets better, so keep reading.

WRITE TO YOUR INNER CHILD

Writing to your inner child is one of the most powerful ways to connect with them. I know it seems a bit strange to write a letter to yourself as a child, but it works and it's worth it. It gives you the chance to say everything you wished your parents had said to you when you were hurting. The exercise of writing a letter to your inner child was developed by world-renowned speaker and author of *You Were Not Born to Suffer,* Blake D. Bauer. The following steps will assist you in writing a letter to your inner child.

What to Say to Your Inner Child

I had no idea what to say when I put pen to paper and tried to write to my inner child. It was such an emotional moment that I was completely lost for words. So, here are some tips to get you started:

I'm Sorry: Hearing your parents say they are sorry for hurting you makes it easier to forgive them because they've acknowledged they were wrong. You would have been so grateful to hear these words as a child, knowing that your parents didn't want to make the same mistakes again.

I Love You: Some parents love their children conditionally—if they get good grades at school, if they do the housework properly, or if they win the trophy on sports day. Remember the days when your parents scolded you for not meeting their standards? They would then ignore you for hours and treat you with contempt until you finally did something right. All you needed to know was that you were loved unconditionally, whether you were performing well or not.

It Wasn't Your Fault: Abused, shamed, or abandoned children believe they are responsible for the treatment they receive. Their inner voice tells them they are not good enough, and that they deserve any punishment they get. You didn't deserve *anything* that happened to you; your parents are to blame. You were the perfect child, but your parents didn't appreciate you.

You Did Your Best: Some parents treat their children as if they're not good enough, no matter how hard they try. They fail to understand that everyone has strengths and weaknesses. A child might be strong in one area, such as math, but not very good at sports. He tries his best, even practicing after school to get his swing right, but nothing seems to work. When his team loses the game, instead of his parents telling him not to worry because he did his best, they scold him for not trying hard enough.

I Forgive You: If your parents blamed you for everything that went wrong in the family, you've most likely carried a burden of shame, believing that whatever you were accused of was your fault. Your parents would blame you if they didn't have enough money to pay the bills, claiming that if they didn't have children, they'd have the things they need. After hearing it was your fault so many times, your parents didn't need to blame you for anything because you blamed *yourself.* Now it's time to forgive yourself for falling for their lies and believing you were to blame for everything.

Thank You: If your inner child hadn't survived the abuse, you wouldn't be here now. So, thank your inner child for being strong and holding on. You could have given up a long time ago, but you chose to keep fighting because you believed it would get better one day. You didn't know when, but your instincts were telling you that your nightmare would one day come to an end.

You can also write a letter to yourself *from* your inner child. This will help you release the negative emotions associated with your childhood trauma. As a child, even if you wanted to tell someone what was going on or how you felt, you were generally not able to articulate yourself in the way you needed to. But you can as an adult. So, write a letter from your inner child to yourself and talk about the pain you felt when you were going through those things.

Step 1: Get a pen and some paper and go somewhere quiet where you can concentrate and won't be distracted.

Step 2: Take several deep breaths while closing your eyes.

Step 3: Imagine that you are somewhere beautiful. How do you feel being there? What is the scenery like? Are there waterfalls? A sunset?

Step 4: Take a seat on a long bench in this wonderful place, and see your inner child walking towards you from a distance. They take a seat next to you.

Step 5: What do you want to say to your inner child, as an adult? What did your parents fail to say to you? Ask your inner child to tell you what he/she needs to know. What could you teach them that would assist in the healing process?

Step 6: When you've thought about what you want to say, start the letter with *Dear [your name]*, and write down all of your inner child's thoughts and feelings. End the letter with *Love [your name]*.

Step 7: Once you've finished writing, take a few deep breaths and lean into the feeling of being able to express yourself clearly during your suffering, and the relief you feel knowing that help is on its way.

Step 8: Write yourself several letters at different times in your life.

EMOTIONAL TRIGGERS AND HOW TO IDENTIFY THEM

Most people are not aware of their emotional triggers until they make a conscious decision to confront them. You may get angry or upset during a conversation because of a random statement someone made. To the person who said it, it may have meant nothing, but it was a trigger for you. Triggers activate our emotions, and when we don't know what our triggers are, we can't control our behavior because the response is unconscious. Once you're exposed to certain words, people, things, colors, smells, or places, you don't think about your reaction—it's automatic. We are also triggered by emotions. If you were raised in a violent household, someone else's anger will trigger you. If your parents didn't allow you to express emotions such as crying, you'll be triggered by crying.

Triggers are connected to our thoughts, memories, and experiences. All of our experiences are stored in the subconscious mind, and when we are faced with something that brings that memory back to life, it triggers us. If you nearly drowned as a child, walking past a pond might trigger you. For example, say your friend surprises you by taking you to the beach for your birthday. But instead of thanking her for this kind gesture, you start screaming at your friend for taking you to the beach without asking you first. You are unaware that water is symbolic of the fear you experienced when you were drowning. Logically, you know that you won't drown as long as you don't go near the water, but in your mind, water represents fear, and anytime you see water, you're afraid. This is how triggers work:

- It starts with a thought, and then an emotion.

- Your past emotions and experiences are connected to your thoughts.

- When you're around someone displaying emotions such as depression or rage, these emotions trigger your thoughts.

- Once you know which thoughts trigger an emotional reaction, you can change your behavior.

Intellectually, you understand that your fear of water is irrational. Since your friend isn't afraid of water, you know there is nothing scary about it, and therefore there must be something else connected to your fear of water.

Exercise to Identify Your Triggers

There are several ways you can get triggered by an emotion, including reading about them. In this exercise, you are going to read through a list of triggers, and your reaction will determine whether it's a trigger to you. Since this is a triggering exercise, if you're not ready to confront your triggers, you might want to skip this section. Get a pen and paper and read through this list. If you experience any intense emotions as you're reading, write down the emotion that triggered it. There may be more than one. For example, if the word *crying* makes you feel angry, write down *crying* and then *angry*.

- Crying
- Misery or unhappiness
- Victim mentality
- Sarcasm
- Anger
- Entitlement
- Sadness or moping
- Arrogance
- Attention-seeking
- Silent treatment
- Nervousness or worry
- Criticizing or judging
- Too intense
- Passive-aggressive
- Blaming
- Aggression or hostility
- Frustration or irritation

- Conceit
- Manipulation
- Being ignored
- Deceit or lying

CONNECTING THE DOTS

If you felt angry when you read the word *crying*, do any memories come up connected to that trigger? You may recall something like crying in front of your mother and, instead of her comforting you, she got angry because you were crying and interrupting her TV show. Write down everything you can remember about these incidents. There is a chance that you won't be able to think of any memories, and if that's the case, there's a possibility you've buried the traumatic incident so deeply, you'll need professional help to retrieve it.

EMOTIONAL TRIGGER REACTIONS

Psychologists are capable of pinpointing emotional triggers because they have common reactions. These include:

Fear: Thoughts that something worse will happen intensify fear.

Frustration or Overwhelm: When you feel responsible for other people's emotions.

Defensiveness or Hostility: When someone accuses you of something that has nothing to do with you.

HOW TO RELEASE EMOTIONAL TRIGGERS

A combination of meditation and yoga will free you from your emotional triggers. Practice these exercises daily, as well as when you're feeling emotionally triggered.

Acceptance Yoga Meditation

Accepting that you feel triggered is a part of the healing process. Instead of running from it, or burying it, acknowledge and accept it.

WARNING: This pose is for those with some yoga experience. If you don't feel flexible enough while following the steps, stop and sit on a yoga block to complete the pose.

- Kneel on the floor with your knees bent and your torso upright. Your feet should be on the side of your thighs.

- Position your hands on the floor next to your thighs and lean backwards while moving your hands in the direction of your buttocks.

- Bend your arms so you're resting on your forearms. If you're sitting on a yoga block, stop here.

- If you're comfortable, lower your back all the way down to the floor.

- Look up at the ceiling and think about your trigger.

- Say these words: "I am feeling triggered because... The discomfort I feel is a part of the healing process, and I accept it."

Mindfulness Meditation

For many of us, being present is an alien concept. We spend our time regretting things we've done in the past, or worrying about what's to come in the future. You will notice this when you start paying attention to your thoughts. These thoughts are a waste of energy because we can't change the past, and nor can we determine what will happen in the future. But what we can do is submerge ourselves in the present moment and enjoy it. You can incorporate mindfulness meditation into your daily routine, but you can also practice it at any time throughout the day when you are emotionally triggered and you feel as if you don't have control over your mind.

- Spend a few seconds taking deep breaths.

- Look around and pay attention to the things you can see, hear, and feel. Is it hot or cold? What do your clothes feel like? Are you eating anything? If so, what does it taste like?

- Now that you're focused on the present, pay attention to your breath and repeat a mantra that reflects your present moment such as, "I can hear the wind blowing through the trees," "I can taste the ham in my sandwich," or, "It's cold in this room."

- Stay in the present moment by repeating the mantra until you feel calm again.

Moving Meditation Practice

When the mind is attacking itself with anxiety, fear, and worry, moving meditation helps stabilize the mind and body, enabling you to become more in tune with your emotions.

- Sit comfortably and pay attention to your breath.

- Stretch your body and remain in that position for 20 seconds.

- Pay attention to the feeling in your body. Is there any tension? If so, breathe into it.

- As you breathe out, surrender to the stretch and let go of the tension.

- Keep breathing at a normal and steady pace.

- Continue stretching and meditating until you feel calm again.

Breath-Counting Meditation

When your mind is all over the place and slowing it down seems impossible, practice breath-counting meditation. By counting and paying attention to your breath, you create distance between your body and your thoughts.

- Sit or lie in a comfortable position.

- Make sure both feet are flat on the floor if seated.

- Inhale deeply and count to one.

- Exhale deeply and count to two.

- Inhale deeply and count to three.

- Exhale deeply and count to four.

- Keep going until you get to 10 and start again, but start by exhaling.

- If you lose count because you stopped paying attention, start again.

- Keep going until you feel peaceful and calm again.

YOGA/MEDITATION FOR SELF-LOVE

If you're not intentional about loving yourself, you'll always be inse-cure because the world we live in doesn't allow us to love ourselves. We are constantly bombarded with images of the perfect life, and if we don't match up, the message is clear: we're not good enough. People only feel good about themselves if they're keeping up with the Joneses—but it eventually becomes exhausting. There is nothing wrong with wanting to live your best life, but when you allow what you own or what you've achieved to define you, you'll never find true happiness because what happens when you lose these things? The negative voice we have within is always trying to steal our joy and convince us to look outside of ourselves for self-worth, but the reality is that if you can't find it within, you'll never have it. Meditation is a great way to condition your mind that you're worthy, that you're good enough, and to fill yourself with the love you deserve. When your emotional triggers attempt to rob you of your self-worth, fight back with meditation:

- Get in a comfortable position, whether sitting or lying down, and turn your palms upwards.

- With your eyes closed, pay attention to your breath.

- Get in tune with your body—are you tense or relaxed? Maintain that feeling in your body.

- Inhale deeply through your nose, and exhale deeply through your mouth several times.

- Focus on your mind and body while breathing. Is there tension in your body? Are you overthinking, or is your mind still? How are your emotions?

- Place both hands over your heart, and continue breathing. What feelings come up as you do this?

- Continue breathing at a normal rhythm and experience the air that flows through your body.

- Breathe out all the negative thoughts and feelings that have hijacked your body.

- After each breath in, say, "I love all of me." After each breath out, say, "There is nothing in life I don't deserve."

- Keep going until you are overcome with peace.

- Visualize yourself in front of a mirror, staring at your reflection. What can you see when you look at yourself? Are you happy, sad, frustrated?

- Even if you don't see anything positive, repeat affirmations that uplift your spirit, such as, "I am an amazing person," "I am a sensational person," or, "I am a fantastic person."

- Imagine taking a deep breath and taking warm love into your heart and letting it fill your entire body.

- Imagine feeling comfort and calm flowing through your body.

- Keep doing this until you feel a sense of overwhelming peace.

YOGA/MEDITATION FOR INNER STRENGTH

One of the greatest downfalls for an empath is that they want to please everyone and they get terribly depressed when they can't. The reality of life is that no matter how nice, talented, or attractive you are, not everyone is going to like you. We waste so much time and energy thinking about who doesn't like us, and what people think about us—when there is absolutely nothing we can do about it. You can't control how people feel about you or treat you. But you *can* control how you react to it. Your focus should be on infusing the world with positive energy and ignoring those who don't enrich your life. One way to achieve this is through connecting with your inner core by strengthening your core muscles. The following yoga poses will help you do this:

Forearm Pose

- Lie face down, stretch your arms out in front of you, and push your chest up off the ground.

- Use your toes and forearms to lift your body off the ground so you're resting on your elbows.

- Remain in this position for 30 seconds.

- Turn your body to the side, lift your arm up towards the ceiling, and use your other arm to balance yourself.

- Remain in this position for 30 seconds.

- Lean over to the other side and follow the same steps.

Side Plank Pose

- Extend your legs outwards while lying on your side.

- Use one arm to lift yourself up off the floor.

- Direct your other arm towards the ceiling and position it under your stomach.

- Place one knee on the ground and remain in the position for 10 seconds.

- Do this five times and move onto the other side.

Breath Retention Pose

WARNING: Be mindful of how you feel while holding your breath. Don't get to the point of lightheadedness headedness before you start breathing.

- Position a yoga block in front of you, lean forward and place your hands on it.

- Use the tips of your toes to push yourself up while inhaling and exhaling deeply.

- Position your feet flat on the floor, inhale deeply and hold your breath for as long as you can.

- As you breathe out, remove your hands from the yoga block, place your head on your knees and take hold of your ankles with both hands.

AFFIRMATIONS FOR INNER CHILD HEALING

Affirmations are a powerful way to reprogram the mind and transition you from a place of insecurity and low self-esteem to a place of empowerment and confidence. I would advise writing out the three affirmations that speak to you the most, then carrying them with you wherever you go, and reading them to yourself several times throughout the day. Additionally, stick them to your mirror, and say them to yourself out loud every morning and night. It will feel very uncomfortable saying these affirming words to yourself because you're not used to speaking to yourself with such kindness. Your inner voice is constantly telling you how worthless you are. However, the only way to disrupt negative self-talk is to replace it with positive self-talk. Here are some affirmations to get you started:

- I feel gratitude because my inner child has helped me find my true and authentic self.

- My childhood trauma is something that happened *to* me—it is not me, it has no power over me, and does not define me.

- I will take my time healing every part of my inner child.

- My inner child will never feel abandoned or neglected again, because we are going through this healing journey together.

- I choose to transfer all my energy into healing my inner child.

- I am teaching myself how to be a better parent by healing my inner child.

- Healing my inner child will empower me to become the best version of myself.

- I am allowed to take on the childlike qualities of carefree living, innocence, and playfulness.

- I am glad to have met my inner child.

- My inner child has a voice and he/she can use it whenever he/she desires.

- I am stronger because I know how to be vulnerable.

- It is a blessing to be unique.

- I am enjoying embracing my inner child.

- I will never ignore the needs of my inner child.

- Being innocent and vulnerable is my new normal.

- My inner child has feelings, and I trust them.

- My inner child is helping me just as much as I am helping him/her.

- I am just as tuned in to the needs of my inner child as I am tuned in to the needs of others.

- I re-parent my inner child with love, compassion, and understanding.

- I love my inner child unconditionally.

- I respect the thoughts and feelings of my inner child.

- I reclaim the innocence of my inner child.

If you've just started dating someone, and you suspect they're a dark empath, they've probably started out by love-bombing you. Keep reading to find out the strategies the dark empath will use to trap you in their web of splendor.

CHAPTER 5:

DARK EMPATHS LOVE-BOMB THEIR WAY INTO YOUR HEART

I spent three years being manipulated and exploited because I didn't know what a dark empath was. I witnessed the traits I am about to detail in my partner firsthand. Initially, I didn't think anything of it, because at the end of the day, no one's perfect. But his behavior became worse and more intense as time went on. You can save yourself a lot of heartache by knowing how to recognize a dark empath.

THEY LOVE-BOMB YOU

The term "love-bombing" first came about in the 1970s. It was coined to describe the tactics used by religious cults to entice people into their organization. It's a form of psychological manipulation used to gain full control over a person. Love-bombing is also a strategy narcissists use to get you addicted to them when they first meet you. Dark empaths do exactly the same thing, and it's one of the reasons I got so caught up in my ex—because he was super romantic. He totally swept me off my feet and it all felt exciting and fun. Having someone drown you in admiration and affection is especially thrilling at the beginning of a relationship. However, love-bombing is a clever form of manipulation that will have you so sprung, you won't realize what's hit you until it's too late. There are several signs that a person is love-bombing you, and these are as follows:

Compliments: They will go so over the top with the compliments that it will sound disingenuous. They might say things like:

- "You are the most beautiful person I've ever seen in my life."

- "Everything about you is just perfect."

- "I can't imagine spending time with anyone else but you."

Gifts: Love-bombers will shower you with luxury gifts and do inappropriate things such as send large bunches of flowers to your workplace. They'll book a vacation without telling you and expect you to drop everything and go. Everyone loves being spoiled—so what's the problem? The problem is that your significant other isn't spoiling you out of the goodness of their heart; it's how they manipulate you into feeling indebted to them.

Communication: They will want to speak to you several times throughout the day and will blow up your phone at every opportunity they can get. I once came out of a meeting to one hundred and two missed calls, and twenty-five text messages from my ex! I quickly realized that he'd intentionally bought me the phone so I would feel obligated to respond when he called. Lopsided communication is a major red flag because normal people communicate like they're playing a game of tennis. If you're feeling overwhelmed by how often they call you, it's a problem.

Commitment: Love-bombers will pressure you into commitment and start planning for the future. They'll start talking about living together or getting married, and they'll say it's because they've fallen in love with you and they need to be with you. It is highly unrealistic to fall in love with someone within a couple of weeks, because strong relationships are developed over time; they don't happen overnight. They will insist you're soulmates and say things like:

- "Destiny brought us together."
- "You are my soul mate."
- "No one understands me more than you."
- "We met just at the right time."

Boundary Violation: If you feel that you need to slow things down because the relationship is going too fast for you, they'll attempt to manipulate you into giving them what they want. They'll get upset if you try to establish boundaries in the relationship. Whatever you say will fall on deaf ears, and they'll continue with their outpouring of love and expect you to accept it.

Needy: You can see a dark empath every day of the week but it still won't be enough. If you don't reply to their text messages within two and a half seconds, they'll get upset. You'll start feeling obligated to give in to their demands because of how well they treat you.

Your Attention: They want to be at the center of your life at all times, and if you're not paying them attention, they'll get mad. If your phone rings when you're together, they'll expect you not to answer it because they don't want you to speak to anyone else. If you do answer it, they'll sulk and make you feel guilty until you get off the phone. Basically, any screen time is a problem when you're together—no texting or scrolling because all eyes must be on them.

Isolation: The love-bomber will demand so much of your time that you won't have any to give to your friends and family. If you make plans with anyone else, they'll make you feel guilty and will try and get you to cancel by saying something like they had a surprise for you. Isolating you from your loved ones is an additional way of controlling you.

How You Will Feel Being Love-Bombed

It will feel awesome at the beginning; you'll have butterflies, and you'll feel all giddy when you're around them. But after a while, you will start feeling suffocated. If the person you're seeing exhibits all the signs of love-bombing, and you start feeling overwhelmed and unbalanced, there's a high chance you're being love-bombed.

Overwhelmed: Real love is gentle, patient, and kind, but dark empaths are so intense, you feel like you're on a speeding train when you're together. They are unpredictable, and you have no idea what their next move will be. During our first week of dating, my ex turned up at my apartment at 3:00 a.m. saying he desperately missed me and needed to see me. I felt pressured to give in to his demands anytime he wanted to see me.

Imbalanced: You will start feeling uncomfortable because the way you're being treated seems too good to be true. This is your intuition telling you something's not quite right. It's normal to have a bit of anxiety when you first start seeing someone because you don't know how things will turn out. However, when you start sensing that something is too good to be true, it usually is.

The love-bombing will stop out of the blue, and you will feel a shift in their energy. They'll become cold and indifferent and you'll think you've done something wrong. They've succeeded in forming an emotional bond with you, and now they will start showing their true colors and manipulating you to get what they want.

INSIDE THE MIND OF A LOVE-BOMBER

Outside of narcissism and dark empaths, love-bombers are typically mentally unstable. They feel inadequate and struggle with extremely low self-esteem. For some people, love-bombing is an unconscious act; it's not planned. It's a behavioral pattern they've adopted because they feel so worthless, they've convinced themselves that loving someone excessively will lead that person to return the love.

THE DANGERS OF LOVE-BOMBING

Love-bombing isn't genuine; it doesn't come from the heart, and there are ulterior motives at work. Because it's about personal gain, they have no real concern for the object of their affection. Their end goal is to capture their victim to have complete control over them. Everyone wants love; it's human nature—and dark empaths know this. They use this knowledge to gain a foothold in the person's life. Here are a few reasons why love-bombing is dangerous:

It's Addictive: Empaths who don't understand their gift are particularly prone to the wiles of a love-bomber because they feed off external validation. Each time the love-bomber compliments us or presents us with a gift, we get a dopamine rush. Love-bombers are also good at showering you with adoration in front of friends and family, which causes them to get excited, which excites *you* even further and feeds the addiction. The dopamine rush gives you a false sense of security because you assume they're going to make you feel like that all the time. But little do you know, it's only temporary. Unfortunately, you've got so used to how the love-bombing makes you feel, that when it's withdrawn, you'll do anything to get it back. And this is where the manipulation begins because they know you'll do anything for it.

Mental Health: The cycle of love-bombing is difficult to break, and this can affect your mental health. It causes anxiety because now you don't know whether your partner is going to hurl insults at you or tell you you're amazing. And love-bombing can cause depression because you're now trapped in an abusive relationship and you don't have the mental capacity to leave.

How to Handle a Love Bomber

Experts advise that you handle love-bombing in the same way you would a busy road. Stop, look, and listen:

- **Stop:** Put the brakes on by telling the person that you really do like them, but things are moving a bit too fast for you and you'd like to slow it down. If you've had a bad relationship that started great and ended badly in the past, you can use that as an excuse.

- **Look:** Pay attention to their behavior; if their words and actions don't line up, that's another red flag.

- **Listen:** The love-bomber will attempt to keep the relationship as it is because slowing things down will spoil their plan. But don't be afraid to challenge them. If they say, "But I was hoping we could move in together soon," reply, "I personally think it's way too early to move in with someone you've only known for [amount of time]." Love-bombers are extremely controlling, and they are not willing to compromise. Additionally, they hate being challenged and will probably reply with something rude, such as, "It's your loss. You'll never find anyone who will love you as much as I do." A comment like this will tell you everything you need to know—and that should be your cue to exit the relationship.

Dark empaths are extremely manipulative, and once they're confident their love-bombing strategy has been successful, their true colors will begin to show—and gaslighting is one of their favorite tactics.

CHAPTER 6:

DARK EMPATHS WILL GASLIGHT YOU

Psychological manipulation comes in many forms, and gaslighting is one of them. It typically occurs in an abusive romantic relationship but it can also take place amongst families, friends, and co-workers. It's a subtle form of abuse that involves the abuser creating a false narrative that forces the victim to question their reality. If the gaslighting goes on long enough, the victim will begin losing confidence in how they perceive their interactions with others, and will start questioning their mental health.

GASLIGHTING TECHNIQUES

My ex-partner was a master gaslighter, and I would often leave our conversations feeling confused. My thoughts were scrambled, and I genuinely thought there was something wrong with me. Here is how a typical gaslighting scenario went with him (this really happened):

Me: "I let my family know you were coming over for Thanksgiving dinner next week and they can't wait to meet you."

James: "When did we have this conversation? The last time we spoke about your family, we agreed that we'd wait until we were confident about the direction our relationship was headed. You know we've been arguing a lot lately. Sometimes I don't know if we're going to last."

Me: "We discussed this two days ago in the car on the way to the grocery store. You said you were nervous about meeting them, and I said you didn't have anything to worry about because my family are really cool people."

James: "That's not how the conversation went. I said I was nervous about meeting them because we argue too much, and I didn't want to disappoint them if we broke up. We agreed to give it another six months before doing the family thing. You must have got it mixed up—you were probably simultaneously thinking about how you can get ahead in your career so you can be better than me. Seriously, this is why I'm worried about us; you can't even do something as simple as concentrate on a conversation."

Did you notice what he did there? He didn't deny that the conversation had happened, but tried to convince me that it had gone in a different direction. He then deflected by changing the focus of the discussion by accusing me of something totally unrelated. So, I'll start with deflection as one of the techniques gaslighters use:

Deflection: Gaslighters will get you to focus on something else so that you lose your concentration and forget about what you wanted to say. Another example of deflection includes refusing to give you a straight answer. If you ask if they've got any plans for Saturday night, they'll respond with something like, "Why is it any of your concern what I'm doing on Saturday night? I'm tired of your controlling behavior— you want to know my every last move and I'm sick of it." The victim asks a simple question that the abuser manages to turn into an attack on their character.

Scapegoating: Scapegoating involves the gaslighter convincing you that the negative outcome was your fault. For example, you arranged to meet up for dinner at 6:00 p.m. after work. Your partner turns up at 7:00 p.m. and, instead of apologizing, claims it's your fault they're late because you called them at work to make sure they were coming so you could book the table. Apparently, your phone call was a distraction and they had to stay later to finish a project. Any sane person can tell that their lateness clearly has nothing to do with you, but they'll try and convince you it was your fault.

Chameleon Tendencies: It's normal to change our behavior depending on the social environment we're in. However, the gaslighter literally becomes a different person depending on who they're around. It's not a slight change in behavior—it's extreme. At home, your partner is rude and cruel to you and doesn't show you any affection. But when the two of you get around friends and family, they treat you like royalty and they're overly affectionate. Everyone thinks you're so lucky and they refer to you as #couplegoals on Instagram posts. This is a dangerous place to be in because your partner is so good at deceiving people, that when you attempt to reach out to your friends and family about the abuse, there's a possibility they won't believe you.

Name-Calling: Name-calling is an effective gaslighting technique because it adds to the victim's low self-esteem. They'll call them names like *stupid*, *useless*, *fat*, and *ugly*. The gaslighter knows exactly when to start hurling this type of abuse, and it's typically when the victim is feeling at their lowest. The idea is to kick them when they're down.

Reality Distortion: Reality distortion involves the abuser convincing the victim they haven't seen what they've seen. I once witnessed James stealing money from my purse. I went upstairs into the bedroom and saw him take the money out of my purse and put it in his pocket. When he turned around and saw me standing there, he said, "Wow, so you're creeping up on me now?" He then proceeded to walk out of the room. I followed him and asked why he had stolen money out of my purse, and he said he didn't know what I was talking about and that I must have been seeing things because he was only moving my bag out of the way so he could get something. When I asked him to empty his pockets, he refused and started accusing me of being controlling. This is a prime example of reality distortion. It's also important to mention that telling white lies is not the same as reality distortion. The most morally upright people tell white lies. The difference between a black and a white lie is that there is no manipulation involved in a white lie; you're not trying to convince a person they're delusional for what they've witnessed you doing.

Trivializing Your Feelings: The gaslighter will act like your feelings don't matter so they can have control over your emotions. When you're speaking to them about something that bothers you, they'll say things like, "You're way too sensitive," "You're being really dramatic right now," or, "You really need to calm down." Statements like this trivialize your feelings and cause you to shut down. After a while, you'll become emotionally indifferent because you're afraid to share how you really feel.

Signs You're a Victim of Gaslighting

My mental health suffered tremendously because of the extreme gaslighting techniques James used on me. It's literally a form of mind control, and it's dangerous. Here are some signs you're a victim of gaslighting:

- **Low Self-Esteem:** For whatever reason, a lot of empaths suffer from low self-esteem. But it will get ten times worse when you're in an abusive relationship. You tolerate the disrespect not only because you have a low opinion of yourself, but because you believe that if you give your partner enough love, they'll change. The abuse continues because your partner takes full advantage of your low self-esteem. You start losing confidence in your abilities, and you reject offers to advance your career, socialize, or grow as a person because you don't feel good enough.

- **You Focus on Your Flaws:** The main aim of an emotional manipulator is to make you believe you're inferior. As you read in the scenario I mentioned, gaslighting always involves convincing you there's something wrong with how you perceived the situation, which implies there is something inherently wrong with you. As a result, you become obsessed with your negative personality traits your abuser keeps highlighting. You start to believe that these flaws make you unlikeable or unlovable, and that you are inherently damaged or a bad person. The ultimate goal of the gaslighter is to keep you totally dependent on them so you won't leave the relationship. They won't need to tell you no one else will want you because *you've* convinced *yourself.*

- **You Are Confused:** Because your brain is always in a state of panic, you feel confused all the time and find it difficult to make even the smallest decisions. You believe you are incapable of making the right choices and will turn to your partner for everything. This gives them even more ammunition to tear you down. Although your abuser is secretly happy that their plan to destroy you is working, they will say things like, "I can't believe how stupid you are. Why is it so hard for you to do something as simple as buy milk from the store?" I used the milk example because any time I bought milk, he complained that I'd bought the wrong brand or the wrong type, despite the fact that he'd specifically told me what to buy. One week I'd buy full-fat milk from Kroger and he'd say, "I don't like full-fat milk from Kroger—I told you to get semi-skimmed milk from Walmart." The next time I went to the store, I'd buy semi-skimmed milk from Walmart and he'd say, "I told you I don't like semi-skimmed milk from Walmart—I told you to get skimmed milk from Target." So the next time, I'd get him to write down the type of milk he wanted, and that would give him the green light to call me stupid.

- **You Don't Recognize Yourself:** You feel like a shadow of your former self. You are well aware that you're not the person you used to be, but you can't figure out why. Everything about you has changed so drastically; you don't dress the same, speak the same, or act the same. Your friends and family even tell you you've changed. But you don't know how to get back to the person you used to be. It's like looking back at a different person.

- **You Lie:** To avoid any form of confrontation, you lie to yourself and others. Your partner will grind you down and make you feel defeated if you challenge them. You've now become terrified of confrontation, and to avoid these feelings, you lie to your abuser, friends, family, and even yourself.

- **You're Uncomfortable:** You feel extremely uncomfortable in the gaslighter's presence. When they walk into a room, you become nervous and tense because you're preparing yourself for something bad. Deep down, you know you need to leave the relationship, but you don't have the mental capacity to do so.

If your partner has started spreading rumors about you, there's a high chance he's a dark empath because that's one of the many ways they control you. In Chapter 7, you'll learn all about why dark empaths spread rumors about their significant others, and how to handle it.

CHAPTER 7:

DARK EMPATHS WILL SPREAD RUMORS ABOUT YOU

W hy would anyone spread rumors about their partner? Aren't they supposed to love each other and be a part of a team? Well, not when you're with a dark empath. When they can't control you, and they don't get what they want, they'll spread malicious rumors about you, sit back and watch the drama unfold—then will be there to comfort you when you're totally broken because of it. But that's exactly what they wanted. Here are some of the main reasons why a dark empath will spread rumors about you:

Jealousy: Jealousy gets problematic when the jealous person becomes controlling and possessive, and this is typically the case in abusive relationships. The abuser will impose double standards on their partner that might include, for example, forbidding them to hang out with the opposite sex alone, despite the fact that it's okay for *them* to do it. They will also start excessively monitoring your communication. They'll want your passwords to your social media accounts so they can check who you're sending direct messages to and whose posts you're liking. They'll be constantly looking over your shoulder while you're texting, and putting their ear to the phone while you're speaking. Extreme jealousy is suffocating, and you'll find yourself submitting to your partner's requests to avoid the hell that comes with not doing what they want. If they've tried every trick in the book to get you to sever ties with your friends but nothing's working, they'll resort to spreading rumors about you.

To Turn People Against You: Dark empaths want to isolate you so you're totally dependent on them. One strategy they use to achieve this is by turning people against you—but they will ensure that they themselves are kept out of the equation. For example, they'll set up a fake social media page and use it to contact your friends. They will then start telling them terrible things that you've done. One of the oldest tricks in the book is to use what you've said about a friend against you. When you told your partner that your best friend had got a new job, you were extremely happy for her and excited about the new journey she was about to embark on. But your partner completely twists what you say and sends a message to your best friend that goes something like this:

"Hey, Jessica, I hope you are well. I know I'm sending you an anonymous message, but I don't want to get involved in any drama so I think it's best I keep my name out of it. We both know Tina, and unfortunately, she's not who she claims to be. I'd been hearing through the grapevine for some time that she was fake and two-faced but I didn't want to believe it until she confirmed it with her own mouth. Last week we went out to dinner, and she told me about your new job (congratulations by the way). She said she doesn't understand how you got such a lucrative role when you're not the smartest person in the world. She was banging on about how you don't even have a degree, you can't articulate yourself properly, and she suspects that you slept with the manager to get the job. I know it hurts to hear that your best friend has said something like this about you, but it's better you know now. The thing is, I've always suspected she was jealous of you so this didn't come as much of a surprise to me. Personally, I've started keeping my distance from her, and I think you should do the same."

The next thing you know, your friend is calling you up to confront you about the message. All you can do is deny it, but a seed of distrust has been sown, and it's only a matter of time before your friendship is completely ruined. The dark empath will sit back and watch how the scenario unfolds.

To Destroy Your Confidence: Everything emotional abusers do is done with a view to destroying your confidence. As mentioned, the goal is for you to be totally dependent on them so they have full control over you. Once you're aware that the rumors are out, you have no way of knowing if people believe them or not. They may tell you they don't believe the rumors because they don't want to make you feel bad, but what if, deep down, they've started doubting you? There are some people who run with everything they're told, and they'll make it obvious they believe the rumors by keeping you at arm's length. Knowing that people have started distancing themselves from you, and not knowing how people truly feel about you will have a negative effect on your self-confidence.

How to Handle Rumors

Having rumors spread around town about you isn't nice. It destroys trust and makes people suspicious of you. If you're anything like me, you'll want to bury your head in the sand and hope the rumors go away. But sometimes you've got to confront them. Here are some tips on how to do so:

Pick Your Battles: If your partner has gone on the warpath and spread several rumors about you, handle the biggest ones and let the small ones die out on their own. Confronting rumors is exhausting, so you'll want to make sure you use your energy wisely.

Don't Let It Get to You: I know this is easier said than done, but you can't afford to let the rumors get to you. Not only for the sake of your mental health, but it will give your abuser the ultimate satisfaction to know you're having a difficult time with the things being spread about you. In fact, the best thing to do is to not say anything about it to your abuser at all. They'll probably bring it up after a few days to taunt you, but maintain a calm disposition. Remember, you are above the rumors, and they are beneath you. Don't give them any power by taking the rumors personally.

Respond Quickly: Have you ever noticed that when a rumor is started by a celebrity and they're quiet about it, everyone assumes they're guilty? Additionally, when you don't shut rumors down, they take on a life of their own and become more exaggerated. Speak to the people you know have heard the rumor and explain that they are false allegations. What you don't want is for people to start confronting you about them, because you'll end up explaining yourself to people who really don't have any business meddling in your affairs anyway.

Ignore the Naysayers: When it comes to rumors, your camp will be split in two. There will be those who feed into the lies, and those who don't. Our tendency is to focus on the people who feed into the lies because we want to prove that it's not true. But that's a waste of time. You see, they're the ones who don't have anything better to do than listen to gossip mills and spread what they've heard. Your true friends are going to listen to what you've got to say, evaluate the situation objectively, and support you.

Don't Keep Bringing It Up: Eventually, the rumors about you will die down and it will be someone else's turn. But while you're waiting for that to happen, you might start getting frustrated because of the traction that these rumors have gained. However, it's important to understand that it takes time for rumors to fade because some people will take great joy in pushing the narrative. Your abuser will most likely be one of them. When you realize that the rumors are still going, you may be tempted to keep trying to put the fire out—but don't waste your energy, because they'll eventually fizzle out on their own.

Most abusers are aggressive, whether it's physical, emotional, or passive. In Chapter 8, you'll learn all about dark empaths and aggression.

CHAPTER 8:

DARK EMPATHS ARE VERY AGGRESSIVE

My ex-boyfriend showed signs of aggression from the beginning of our relationship, but, as a typical empath, I ignored the warning signs until I ended up with a black eye. The first time I realized he had a bad temper, we were out at a restaurant and the waiter brought him the wrong food. Instead of politely asking for the meal he'd ordered, he smashed the plate on the floor and walked out. The scary thing was that he was extremely calm about it, and when we left the restaurant, he acted as if nothing had happened. He didn't mention it—he just took me out to dinner somewhere else.

WHAT IS AGGRESSION?

Aggression refers to behavior that results in psychological and physical harm to others, yourself, objects, or the environment. Everyone feels like being aggressive at times, but most refrain from taking it out on other people. Instead, they'll play sports, or go to the gym for relief. Extreme or pervasive aggression may be a sign of an undiagnosed mental health condition, a medical issue, or substance abuse.

AGGRESSION—WHAT ARE THE SIGNS?

Most aggressive behaviors are obvious. When someone starts getting loud and obnoxious, others will typically jump in to defuse the situation. However, passive aggression is very subtle and difficult to detect. Signs of aggression include:

- **Physical:** Physical aggression involves hitting, beating, or kicking another person. It also involves damaging property.

- **Verbal:** Verbal aggression includes yelling, name-calling, and mocking.

- **Relational:** Relational aggression involves sabotaging another person's relationship by doing things like spreading rumors or telling lies about someone.

- **Passive-Aggressive:** Passive aggression involves offering backhanded compliments, or ignoring someone at a social gathering or on social media. The intention is to allow harm to come to a person, instead of harming them directly.

TYPES OF AGGRESSION

According to psychologists, there are two main types of aggression: impulsive aggression, and instrumental aggression.

Impulsive Aggression: Also known as reactive or affective aggression, impulsive aggression is triggered by strong emotions, with anger and jealousy being the most common. This type of aggression happens without warning. Road rage is a good example of impulsive aggression. A person can be singing along to the music in their car, when another car pulls out in front of them. Without thinking about it, their immediate response is to start shouting at the other driver.

Instrumental Aggression: Instrumental aggression is strategic; it is carefully planned over a period of time to achieve a greater goal. For example, when a thief decides to commit a robbery, the greater goal is to get money. But to get the money, the thief is forced to hurt someone.

What Causes Aggression?

Experts have yet to come up with a specific theory on the causes of inappropriate or excessive aggression. But they do believe a number of factors are involved, including biological, psychological, and environmental.

Biological: It is possible that there are hormonal and genetic factors that influence aggression; for example, hormonal imbalances in cortisol and testosterone, or imbalances in neurotransmitters such as dopamine and serotonin. Genetics may play a role in these imbalances. Additionally, experts have found that aggression is linked to brain structure. People with a dysfunctional amygdala have been found to be more aggressive than others.

Psychological: Aggressive behavior is linked to a number of mental health conditions such as:

- Post-traumatic stress disorder (PTSD)
- Narcissism
- Borderline personality disorder (BPD)
- Bipolar disorder
- Attention-deficit/hyperactivity disorder (ADHD)

Psychosis, dementia, epilepsy, brain injuries, and substance abuse can all contribute to aggressive behavior.

Environmental: Being raised in a violent and hostile environment can play a role in a person's tendency to display aggressive behavior because they are more likely to believe that aggression is socially acceptable. Experiencing childhood trauma such as sexual, physical, or emotional abuse can also cause aggression.

If your partner is aggressive, I would advise that you leave the relationship now. If you've just started dating someone, and they appear to have aggressive tendencies, I would advise that you cut them off immediately. This may sound harsh, but trust it's for your own good. As mentioned, James showed his aggressive side very early on, but I chose to ignore it because I thought I could help him. The end result was that he physically abused me. I'm lucky that it was a one-off and that things didn't get any worse. But there are too many people (men and women) who have suffered or lost their lives at the hands of their violent partners to warrant *anyone* staying with an aggressive person.

Does your partner shut down or change the direction of the conversation when an emotionally charged subject comes up? If so, you are probably dealing with an emotionally unavailable person, which is one of the many character traits of a dark empath.

CHAPTER 9:

DARK EMPATHS ARE EMOTIONALLY UNAVAILABLE

To sustain an emotional bond in a relationship, you need to be emotionally available. Without an emotional connection, it's impossible to have a healthy relationship. If you've been dating your dark empath partner for a while, you may have noticed that something just doesn't seem right. They get uncomfortable when discussing emotional experiences. They might walk out of the room, or steer the conversation in another direction. There are several characteristics that make a person emotionally unavailable. Here are some of them:

EMOTIONALLY UNAVAILABLE—WHAT ARE THE SIGNS?

It can be difficult to pinpoint emotional unavailability in dark empaths because in general, emotionally unavailable people know how to make you feel good about yourself and the relationship. They can be very charming and will say all the right things, but you'll never have an intimate connection with them because they don't have the ability to connect in this way. Signs that a person is emotionally unavailable include the following:

You Do All the Work: Despite the fact that emotionally unavailable people have the gift of the gab, when it comes to maintaining the relationship, you do all the work. They seem to enjoy spending time with you, as long as you're the one doing all the planning, texting, and calling. If *you* don't take the initiative, *they* won't. When you're not together, they won't contact you, or they'll take forever to reply to text messages or they won't reply at all, especially to sentimental ones.

They Are Unreliable: They cancel plans or they turn up so late there was no point in them turning up at all. This is an indirect way of keeping a person at arm's length. Your partner will apologize profusely, but they care more about *their* needs and don't want to restructure their lives to include you. Basically, an emotionally unavailable person is not willing to compromise.

They Mirror Your Feelings: How does your partner respond when you share your emotions? Do they mirror yours, or do they express how they truly feel? Talking about emotions is important in a relationship so that both parties can connect on an emotional level. But if your partner shuts down during an intimate conversation or when you ask them direct questions, you are most likely dealing with an emotionally unavailable person.

There Is No Growth: After the love-bombing stage ends, there is no relationship growth. Every so often, they'll tell you they enjoy spending time with you, but that's about it. They don't reveal their vulnerabilities or allow you to see them for who they really are. Your partner is very distant, and you are doing everything you can to form a deeper connection, but nothing seems to work.

They Never Say "Relationship": Emotionally unavailable people usually fear intimacy and commitment. They will act as if they're in a relationship, as in go on dates, meet each other's friends, and spend the night together, but they refuse to talk about being official. Emotionally unavailable people are fine with casual dating, but as soon as you start talking about getting serious, they get uncomfortable.

They Don't Compromise: When you *do* see each other, they decide how you're going to spend your time, and that typically involves doing something *they* usually do. They'll watch their favorite Netflix show, even if you're not interested in it. Or they'll watch their favorite sports team. They may even spend the night playing computer games. When you don't want to do what *they* want to do, they get irritated, and they never ask if there's anything *you'd* like to do.

THE ROOT CAUSE OF EMOTIONAL UNAVAILABILITY

Emotional unavailability can be due to a number of factors, including the following:

Attachment Issues: When parents don't invest in the emotional well-being of their children, it can cause emotional unavailability. Detachment becomes the norm, and they avoid emotional attachments with romantic partners.

A Previous Bad Relationship: A broken heart can make it difficult to express vulnerability with another partner.

Temporary Circumstances: People suffering from mental health conditions such as depression may find it difficult to have an emotional connection with their partner during a depressive episode. Others might not be emotionally available because they are focused on their career or education.

Now What?

If your dark empath partner expresses the need for change, you can help them get through the perils of emotional unavailability. As you've read, there are complex issues involved that are not going to disappear overnight; therefore, your partner must be willing to put the work in. Nevertheless, here are some tips to assist them in overcoming their challenges:

Identify the Root Cause: It will be easier to identify the root cause if your partner's emotional unavailability is connected to a previous relationship or temporary circumstances. However, if it is rooted in childhood trauma and abuse, it will be more difficult to pinpoint. If that's the case, you may need to start by seeing a therapist.

Practice Vulnerability: Your partner can practice vulnerability by opening up more. Start with small things, and when they feel comfortable, they can open up about deeper issues. There are several ways your significant other can practice being vulnerable. These include:

- Journaling feelings.

- Using music or art to practice emotional expression.

- Speaking to trusted people such as family members and close friends about emotions.

- As a couple, start by sharing vulnerabilities and emotional issues via letter or through text messages.

Work Together: When you have an emotionally unavailable partner, you'll eventually get tired of doing all the work and will shut down too. At this point you might as well call it quits if you're both going to avoid matters of the heart. So before this happens, commit to working with your partner to resolve their issues with emotional unavailability.

Mirror Other Couples: If your partner's parents didn't have a healthy relationship, they will have no idea what one looks like. Do you know any couples in healthy relationships? This could be your parents, siblings, or friends. Spend more time with them because this can help your partner learn what a healthy relationship looks like.

Don't Rush: Your partner won't overcome their issues with emotional unavailability overnight; it will take a while—and it's important that you understand this. I know you want to be in a normal, healthy relationship ASAP, but you'll need to work at your partner's pace and not yours. Some days, they'll shut down; others they'll open up. Please keep in mind that healing is not a process you can rush.

If you've never received an apology from your partner, you are most likely dealing with a person who doesn't take responsibility for their actions. You can read all about the signs in Chapter 10.

CHAPTER 10:

DARK EMPATHS DON'T TAKE RESPONSIBILITY FOR THEIR ACTIONS

E motionally immature people don't take personal responsibility for their actions. They either refuse to acknowledge them, or they play the blame game. Dark empaths are renowned for being emotionally immature, and I never once heard my partner accept his wrongdoing for anything. As mentioned, it was always either my or someone else's fault, or he ignored the situation altogether. The truth is that no one likes admitting they've made a mistake because it makes them seem inadequate in some way. But that's how you grow as a person, and growth is always going to be painful. Dealing with a partner who doesn't take responsibility for their actions can be terribly frustrating.

TAKING PERSONAL RESPONSIBILITY—WHY IS IT IMPORTANT?

Life is about learning, applying what you've learned, and evolving. Without applying what we've learned, we will never evolve and become the people we are destined to become. Taking personal responsibility is a form of self-awareness; it shows you are in tune with who you are. When you acknowledge your mistakes, you believe that change is possible. People who are in denial of their mistakes have no interest in changing and making their lives better.

Admitting your mistakes is important in a relationship because it helps to repair the damage you've caused and builds trust. On the other hand, refusing to accept responsibility destroys trust and creates hostility in a relationship. Before I discuss how to cope with a person who avoids taking responsibility for their actions, it's important to understand why they do it.

WHY PEOPLE FIND IT DIFFICULT TO ACCEPT PERSONAL RESPONSIBILITY

While there is a plethora of reasons as to why people don't accept personal responsibility. Some of the most common include:

Inability to Change: Research suggests that people are more likely to admit their mistakes when they believe they can change. In programs such as Alcoholics Anonymous, patients are not permitted to join if they can't admit they have an addiction.

Shame: The overwhelming feeling of distress or embarrassment caused by shame makes people shut down, lie, hide, or deny their behavior in order to minimize the pain associated with the mistake.

Perfectionism: You can read more about perfectionism in Chapter 20. Perfectionists have difficulty admitting their mistakes because they have unrealistically high standards for themselves. They measure their self-worth according to their achievements and performance, so acknowledging their mistakes means they are admitting they are not perfect, which can be extremely traumatic for them. Additionally, their all-or-nothing thinking makes small mistakes look huge, leading a perfectionist to feel like a major failure.

Trauma: Unresolved trauma causes people to see themselves as victims. Painful rejection, betrayal, or criticism can cloud a person's judgment because they are so focused on their emotional pain, they become blind to how their behavior affects others. People who were severely punished, ignored, or blamed for their mistakes during childhood avoid confronting their mistakes, as a subconscious response to this trauma.

A Feeling of Entitlement: Dark empaths believe they are superior to others and therefore have the right to do what they want without suffering the consequences. However, this is typically an unconscious response to overcompensate for insecurity, low self-esteem, or self-doubt.

HOW TO HANDLE PEOPLE WHO WON'T TAKE PERSONAL RESPONSIBILITY

Being in a relationship with someone who won't take personal responsibility is extremely frustrating. You can clearly see that your partner is the problem, but they refuse to acknowledge it. So, how do you handle them? Here are some tips:

Don't Take the Blame: Sometimes, it's easier to accept responsibility for your partner's mistakes and move on than to get them to see the writing on the wall. But by adopting this coping mechanism, you're not helping anyone; in fact, you'll make the situation a lot worse because your partner will know they can shift the blame when it suits them and you'll accept it. Besides, if you want your significant other to change, you can't keep making excuses for them. Some empaths are codependent and will make excuses for their partner, or will try and fix their problems.

Communication Skills: When your partner doesn't take personal responsibility for their actions, you'll find yourself having the same conversations over and over again. It's like speaking to a brick wall; you just can't get through to them. You end up having very emotionally charged arguments, and the problem never gets resolved. But if you, as the most rational person in the partnership, improve your partner's communication skills, you might get a different response. Now, I am in no way suggesting you do all the work here. However, what you're doing is indirectly teaching your partner how to communicate, in the hope that you'll be able to have an intellectual conversation with your significant other about their behavior.

Self-Compassion: When dealing with a situation like this, it's important to understand that you are not to blame. Dark empaths are good at blame-shifting, and they'll make you feel that the relationship could improve if only you were to do better. But *you're* not the problem—*they* are. One way to deal with the pain of having a partner who won't take responsibility for their actions is to show yourself plenty of self-compassion. Here are a few tips:

- **Treat Yourself:** Do something nice for yourself by giving yourself a treat. It might be a long soak in the bath with a glass of wine, or a night out at the movies. Whatever you choose to do, I suggest treating yourself once a week, because it will make your situation a lot more tolerable.

- **Congratulate Yourself:** When you're in a difficult relationship, it's easy to focus on the things that your partner thinks you're doing wrong. As hard as it will be, ignore the negative things they say about you, focus on the things you know you're doing right, and congratulate yourself.

- **Speak to Someone:** You don't possess superhuman strength; you can't do everything on your own, and sometimes you need help. Therefore, confide in a trusted friend or family member about your situation. When you can have an honest conversation with someone about what you're going through, it lightens the load.

As I've mentioned, dark empaths are corrupted empaths. Childhood trauma is the root cause of the problems they have, which include anxiety, depression, codependency, and addiction. In the next three chapters, we will take a look at how these conditions affect dark empaths.

CHAPTER 11:

ANXIETY AND DARK EMPATHS

With an estimated 284 million Americans suffering from anxiety, research suggests it's the most common mental health condition in the United States (as stated by the Anxiety and Depression Association in America). Nevertheless, anxiety is a normal feeling, and most people experience it at some point in their lives. A person can be anxious about taking a test, getting married, or moving into a new house. Temporary anxiety is not a cause for concern; however, continuous feelings of anxiety *are*, and this is what a lot of dark empaths deal with. It's easy to confuse anxiety and depression because they have similar symptoms. The typical symptoms of anxiety include:

- A fear of socializing
- Difficulty breathing
- Feeling nervous
- Fatigue
- Excessive heartrate
- Overthinking
- Difficulty sleeping
- Anxiety attacks
- Excessive sweating

- Easily irritated
- A tingling feeling
- Dry mouth
- Feeling afraid

ANXIETY ATTACK—WHAT IS IT?

A person may have an anxiety attack when they're stressed about life circumstances or fearful about a future event. It's also important to mention that an anxiety attack is not the same as a panic attack. An anxiety attack happens after you've spent time worrying about something. A panic attack happens randomly—you could be on your way to the store not thinking about anything in particular and have a panic attack. Stress and fear are similar in that they involve continuously thinking about the worst-case scenario, and this is what leads to feelings of anxiety. An anxiety attack can last for several hours, and sometimes for months.

WHY DARK EMPATHS SUFFER FROM ANXIETY

Dark empaths suffer from anxiety because, like empaths, they overthink everything. But one of their main concerns is that they'll get found out and their dark side will be exposed. It's an interesting dichotomy: They are attracted to weak empaths because they're easy to manipulate, but weak empaths are the very people who will see them for who they really are. That's one of the main reasons James did not want me to tap into my personal power. When I started my healing journey, he did everything he could to stop me. I didn't understand it at the time, but he knew that, once I became who I was destined to be, things would drastically change in our relationship, and he wasn't ready for that. Additionally, James would get anxious when he was around other anxious people, such as true empaths; he would absorb their energy and carry it with him because he didn't know how to protect himself.

How to Alleviate Anxiety

If anxiety is disrupting your life, I recommend you see a mental health professional. But it's also possible to manage your anxiety without professional help. Here are some tips:

Diet: Without creating an exhaustive list of what to eat and what not to eat, diet plays a major role in anxiety. Research suggests that excessive coffee-drinking triggers anxiety. Sugar and highly processed foods also contribute to the condition. Do your best to eliminate these foods from your diet and replace them with whole foods such as fresh fruits and vegetables, whole-wheat bread, rice and pasta, fish, chicken, and dairy products. If you're a coffee drinker, replace it with green tea.

Sleep: Experts recommend getting between seven and eight hours of sleep a night. Anything less than this can cause irritability, moodiness, and brain fog. Go to bed and wake up at the same time every day. When your body adapts to your routine, you'll start feeling tired at the same time, which will help you sleep better.

Triggers: Increasing your self-awareness will help combat your anxiety by alerting you to your triggers. A good way to do this is to start writing a journal and make a note of the times you feel anxious throughout the day. For example, if you start feeling anxious after drinking a cup of coffee, you know that coffee is a trigger and you can't drink it. If you start feeling anxious while watching your favorite murder-mystery series, you know that the show is a trigger and you can't watch it.

Deep Breathing: If you pay attention to your breathing when you're anxious, you'll notice you take quick, shallow breaths. Shallow breathing makes anxiety worse by causing increased heart rate, muscle tension, and dizziness. When you start feeling anxious, take deep breaths to help calm you down. There are several breathing techniques you can try out to see which one works best for you:

4-7-8 Breathing: This is a famous breathing technique practiced by the Navy SEALs to help them stay calm, focused, and stress-free when entering a dangerous situation. Follow these steps:

- Position the tip of your tongue on the roof of your mouth between your teeth and gums.

- Make a "whoosh" sound while breathing out through your mouth.

- With your mouth closed, breathe in through your nose while counting to four.

- Count to seven while holding your breath.

- Breathe out through your mouth while making a "whoosh" sound, and count to eight.

Box Breathing: Not only does box breathing relieve anxiety and stress, it also helps improve concentration and performance.

- Breathe out while counting to four.

- Don't breathe for four seconds.

- Breathe in for four seconds.

- Hold your breath for four seconds.

- Repeat the process until you stop feeling anxious.

Belly Breathing: The American Institute of Stress recommends 20-30 minutes of belly breathing a day to relieve anxiety and stress.

- Sit or lie in a comfortable position and place one hand on your stomach underneath the rib cage and the other on your chest.

- Relax your stomach completely.

- Take a slow, deep breath in through your nose. You should feel your abdomen rise.

- Purse your lips slightly and take a slow, deep breath out. The hand on your chest should remain still.

Lion's Breath: This breathing technique helps relieve stress by relaxing the muscles in the face and jaw. This exercise is most effective when done in a seated position. Follow these steps:

- Lean forward and rest your hands on the floor or your knees.

- Spread your fingers out in a weblike position.

- Take a deep breath through your nose.

- Open your mouth as wide as possible and stick your tongue out, stretching it downwards towards your chin.

- Push your breath out from the back of your throat.

- From deep within your stomach, make a "ha" sound.

- Let your breath return to normal.

- Repeat 7-10 times.

Mindful Breathing: This technique involves focusing on your breath and the present to keep your mind from drifting off to the past or the future. You can practice this exercise at any time. Follow these steps:

- Choose something calming to focus on, such as a positive word (e.g., *love*), a phrase (e.g., *breathe in peace, breathe out chaos*), or a sound (e.g., *om*).

- Silently repeat your calming focus as you take slow, deep breaths.

- Allow your body to relax into your breathing.

- When your mind drifts, take a deep breath, bring your attention back to your calming focus, and start again.

Resonance Breathing: Resonance breathing will help reduce anxiety by getting you into a relaxed state. Follow these steps:

- Lie in a comfortable position and shut your eyes.

- With your mouth closed, take a soft breath in through your nose.

- Without filling up your lungs, count to six.

- Repeat the breathing exercise for ten minutes.

- Focus on your body and how it feels.

Use Aromatherapy: Carry a bottle of essential oil such as sandalwood, chamomile, or lavender around with you. Anytime you feel anxious, pour a couple of drops on a handkerchief and inhale it. The soothing properties in the oil will calm you down immediately.

Go for a Walk: If you find yourself in a situation where you start feeling anxious, walk away from the situation. As you are walking, focus on something other than the situation that made you anxious. Pay attention to the birds, the cars driving past, or what you're going to eat for dinner.

The 333 Rule: The 333 rule will help calm you down and ground you when you're feeling anxious. It involves doing the following:

- Naming three things you can see

- Describing three sounds you can hear

- Touching or moving three things

Dark empaths are also prone to depression. In Chapter 12, we'll look at some of the symptoms and how to overcome them.

CHAPTER 12:

DEPRESSION AND DARK EMPATHS

The pressures of taking on and dealing with feelings that don't belong to them is a huge burden for dark empaths. When they don't understand their gift, it causes confusion and despair. Dark empaths are often stressed out because they feel as if they're just existing and not living, and they're not conscious of how other people's energy affects them. One way they deal with this is to isolate themselves from the world; this is something that dark empaths do a lot. Because they typically enjoy being around people, their nervous system gets overloaded pretty quickly, and they need to retreat in order to recharge. If you notice this pattern in your partner, it's likely they are depressed. Keep an eye out for the main symptoms of depression, which include:

- Feelings of emptiness, tearfulness, sadness and hopelessness

- Frustration, irritability, or angry outbursts over minor issues

- Loss of pleasure or interest in activities such as sports, hobbies, and sex

- Sleep disruption—sleeping too much, or not sleeping enough

- A lack of energy or tiredness, making it impossible to perform small tasks

- Weight loss due to no appetite, or weight gain due to excessive eating

- Restlessness, agitation, and anxiety

- Slowed speaking, thinking, or body movements

- Feelings of guilt, worthlessness, self-blame, or preoccupation with past failures

- Difficulty making decisions, concentrating, thinking, or remembering things

- Frequent suicidal thoughts, obsession with death

- Physical problems such as headaches and back pain

HOME REMEDIES FOR DEPRESSION

For some people, depression can become so bad that it interferes with everyday activities. If you find yourself unable to function at school or at work, you will need professional help. Additionally, if you experience any of the symptoms mentioned, book an appointment with your doctor for a diagnosis. Whether the doctor diagnoses you with mild or severe depression, you can still use these home remedies in conjunction with the doctor's recommendations, which might include medication.

Get into a Routine: Humans are creatures of habit, and when our lives have no order, it intensifies depression. According to psychiatrist Ian Cook, establishing a solid routine is the first step to overcoming depression. Depression causes life to become overcast, with sufferers becoming unaware of which day of the week it is because all days blur into one. Getting some structure into your life will help pull you out of the rut you're in.

Set Small Goals: The feelings of hopelessness that accompany depression lead to people feeling as if they can't achieve anything, and so they don't bother trying. You might stop doing the dishes or laundry, or even all housework. If you've reached this stage and your house is a mess, commit to doing one thing every two days to get your house back in order.

Exercise: Many psychologists will recommend exercise as a treatment for depression because it triggers the release of feel-good hormones. Decide what type of exercise you're going to do and stick to it daily. Moving your body for 30 minutes a day is all it takes to help manage depression. You could go for a brisk walk, a run, or, if you're feeling up to it, join a gym.

Healthy Eating: As mentioned, one of the symptoms of depression is overeating or undereating. Neither of these are good for you. The best way to manage your eating habits is to eat three healthy meals per day. Even if you don't feel like eating, eat anyway, because the nutrients will fuel your system and give you the energy you need to get through the day.

COPING TECHNIQUES FOR RUMINATING THOUGHTS

Ruminating thoughts are the hallmark of depression, and they're hard to get out of once the cycle starts. The key is to stop them immediately before they intensify. In the same way it's easier to stop a ball from rolling down the hill when you catch it at the top of the hill, it's easier to stop ruminating thoughts when they first enter your mind. Here are some tips to help put a stop to ruminating thoughts:

1. **Challenge Your Thoughts:** People ruminate when they feel responsible for something bad that has happened, or they think they've made a terrible mistake. When the troubling thought arises, challenge it by asking yourself questions such as, "How are these negative thoughts helping me?" and, "Is there any point in me thinking about the past when I can't change it?" Once you start asking yourself questions and answering them, you'll realize that your thought process is irrational.

2. **Make a Plan:** Once you catch the thought, write it down and brainstorm how you're going to resolve it. Write down the steps you'll need to take to resolve the issue, and be as detailed as possible. It's also important that your expectations are realistic, or it will add to your anxiety. Making a plan will get the thought out of your head and enable you to focus on the solution instead of the problem. Once you've got the plan down pat, start taking the required action to resolve it.

3. **Distract Yourself:** Break the thought cycle by distracting yourself and focusing on something else. Quickly scan your environment and choose something else to do, such as phone a friend, watch a movie, do some housework, read a book, or go for a walk.

4. **Set Realistic Goals:** As mentioned, empaths are perfectionists and they ruminate when things don't go according to plan. One of the reasons things might not work out is because your goals are unrealistic. There's nothing wrong

with dreaming big; in fact, I encourage it. The problem is that sometimes, those goals are set without thinking them through or setting reasonable deadlines. To prevent ruminating thoughts about your goals, go through them again and make sure they've been properly thought out. Then give yourself a deadline that you know you'll be able to meet. It's better to have too much time than not enough.

5. **Know Your Triggers:** Whenever you catch yourself ruminating, pay attention to what you're doing at the time. This includes whether you're with someone, you're alone, in bed, the time of day, or where you are.

Mindful Acceptance: Acceptance is a powerful way to practice mindfulness. Acceptance is about acknowledging your feelings without labeling them as good or bad. For example, when you feel anxious or depressed, the natural reaction is to avoid the unpleasant feeling. This seems like the logical thing to do because you don't want to experience it. Therefore, you distract yourself, ignore it, or even turn to alcohol or drugs as a form of escapism. Avoidance might work temporarily, but it's not a long-term solution. Avoidance causes you to fight with the experience as you attempt to run away from it. The feelings will literally chase you, and by running, you are doing yourself further damage. The solution is to acknowledge the thoughts, and then accept them for what they are. You can achieve this by saying out loud, "Thinking is natural," or, "I am thinking right now." This process changes the experience, and research suggests that it changes the feeling associated with the thought.

Relax into the discomfort by leaning into it while paying attention to your breath. Breathe at your normal pace and experience the sensation of breathing. Each time you breathe out, move closer to the sensation of discomfort and imagine the tension diminishing.

Acceptance is also about accepting your situation and accepting where you are in life at that moment. Think about it like this: if you get lost in a forest and you have a map showing your final destination, you'll never get there if you don't know where you are. The next step is frustration, because even though you have your hands on the very thing that can get you where you need to go, you can't follow it. In other words, you may know where you want to go in life, but by avoiding your pain and hoping it will just go away, you're creating emotional blockages that will eventually prevent you from moving forwards.

Avoidance intensifies your suffering because while you're trying to run from your pain, you're also plagued with thoughts such as, "Why am I going through this?" and, "This is so unfair." This struggle gets worse the more you avoid your emotions. Here are some tips on how to cultivate acceptance:

- Name the experience you're trying to avoid. For example, if you feel sad but you're trying to suppress it, say to yourself, "At this moment, I feel sad." Keep repeating it until you've acknowledged how you feel.

- Pay attention to your body—where do you feel the most tension? Think about your breath traveling in and out of the tight area. As you exhale, say to yourself, "The feeling is already here and I'm okay with it."

- Rate your acknowledgement of your current feeling on a scale of one to ten. The aim is to get you to fully accept your feelings. So, ask yourself what you would need to do to increase the number by one. Apply it, and then keep asking yourself the question until you reach ten.

- Ask questions about your experience: "Why do I feel this way?" "When did I start feeling this way?" The more curious you become about your feelings, the easier it will be to accept them.

See a Therapist: If you're feeling completely overwhelmed and can't see a way out of your mental anguish, get professional help.

Dark empaths are also prone to codependency. In Chapter 13, we'll look at some of the symptoms and how to overcome them.

CHAPTER 13:

CODEPENDENCY AND HOW TO OVERCOME IT

When a person is emotionally, mentally, physically, and spiritually reliant on someone, it's referred to as codependency. This type of relationship is most common between romantic partners, but it also exists among friends and family members. Codependency is also common when one person in the relationship is addicted to drugs or alcohol. In fact, according to psychologist Dr. Renee Exelbert, the term first came about in the 1950s in relation to Alcoholics Anonymous. It was used to describe friends and family who support addicts, and how their lives become intertwined in the toxicity of the addiction. Codependency is not a mental illness; therefore, there is no diagnosis for it. But it is a symptom of dependent personality disorder.

CODEPENDENCY AND ITS CAUSES

According to counselor Dr. Mark Mayfield, the root cause of codependency is low self-worth, the inability to set boundaries, and the inability to reject people and have a strong opinion. Additionally, research suggests that there are psychological, biological, and social reasons for codependency.

- **Psychological:** Childhood trauma as a result of emotional abuse or neglect can lead to codependency.

- **Biological:** An underdeveloped prefrontal cortex can lead to the brain's inability to suppress empathic responses. Having too much empathy can lead to a person becoming codependent.

- **Social:** Being raised in an environment with drug-addicted or alcoholic parents can result in codependency.

CODEPENDENCY AND ITS SIGNS

There are several signs that suggest a person is codependent. These include the following:

- They say "yes" to everything.

- They don't trust their abilities.

- They allow others to take advantage of them.

- They don't have a sense of self.

- They take on the responsibilities of others.

- They fear abandonment.

- They are obsessed with approval.

- They have low self-esteem.

- They find it difficult to express themselves.

- They struggle to identify their feelings.

Why Dark Empaths Are Prone to Codependency

Codependency starts during childhood when children tune into the energy of their parents and feel that they need to mirror it to please them. Some empath children unconsciously parent their parents because the parents carry unresolved trauma, are emotionally imbalanced, or have weak personal energetic boundaries. The child connects with the inner life and emotions of their parents, which can lead to the child feeling responsible for their well-being. For example, they may believe that their parents would love them more if they were more intelligent, quiet, sweeter, or calmer. They can also take on the burden of the worry, pain, and fear of their parents. The child feels so uncomfortable with these emotions that they do everything in their power to make their parents happy. This is the root cause of codependency. The child becomes the caregiver and keeps track of their parents' mental, emotional, and energetic states. For example, when their parents return home from work, the child immediately tunes into their energy and adjusts accordingly. This is the start of the child disconnecting from their inner life and their feelings, because when the parents are around, the focus is not on the child's needs. Instead, the child is always focused on the parents and their needs, and is constantly adapting to suit them.

This is also the beginning of fatigue syndrome and people-pleasing. You are so concerned about the well-being of others that you neglect your own needs. This leads to insecurity, low self-esteem, and the need for constant validation. Now you seek inner value from the people in your environment to fill the emptiness inside. If you were always responsible for your parents' emotional state, you will continue living this way subconsciously throughout adulthood.

Codependent empaths experience greater hardships because they live disconnected from themselves and they don't have boundaries. Because of their highly sensitive nature, they're more likely to attract abusive people due to the following:

- They want intimacy and love but they struggle to receive it because of shame.

- They are in tune with the suffering of the abuser and confuse it with love.

- Narcissists, addicts, and people with personality disorders seek out empaths for their kind and giving nature.

- Narcissists see empaths as the perfect victim because they are willing to give them the attention they crave. They are an easy source of narcissistic supply.

- Empaths desire to heal and help troubled people in pain.

- They don't protect themselves because they have no boundaries.

- They absorb negative energy and don't realize where it's coming from.

- They ignore their own feelings and needs in favor of others.

- They believe they can change people and therefore live in a state of denial, despite the evidence confronting them.

- They blame themselves for the way people feel and behave.

- They tolerate abuse because they're so forgiving.

- They understand what people are going through, which leads to denial of abuse.

How to Overcome Codependency

Codependency is learned behavior; therefore, it can be unlearned, but it's not going to happen overnight. Here are some tips on how to overcome codependency:

Healthy Self-Talk: The first step is to change the relationship you have with *yourself*. Codependent people have a terrible inner dialogue. Think about it like this: would you speak to someone you love the way you speak to yourself? You've most likely answered *no* to this question. If you don't love yourself, you can't expect anyone else to love you. By changing your critical and judgmental self-talk to a more understanding and kind one, you'll start feeling better about yourself. Once you start feeling better about yourself, codependency will lose its hold over your life.

Let Go of Control: A codependent person is controlling because that's how they feel loved and safe. But controlling someone is exhausting; by investing all your time and energy in watching your partner's every move and trying to control the outcome of the things they do, you end up burned out. It's important to understand that the only person you can control is *yourself*, and to overcome codependency, you'll need to redirect your energy and your focus back to yourself.

Accept Your Emotions: Codependent people lose touch with their emotions because they're so invested in other people. Learning to become more aware of and accepting your emotions will help you disconnect from everyone else so you can focus on yourself.

Dark empaths are also prone to addiction. In Chapter 14, we'll look at some of the symptoms and how to overcome them.

CHAPTER 14:

DARK EMPATHS AND THE ADDICTION TRAP

We live in an excessively busy and overcrowded world, and we're expected to conform to its norms and values or we're seen as outcasts. If we're not ripping and running during the week, and hitting the town on the weekends, we're frowned upon. Listen to the conversations at work on Monday mornings; they are full of tales of drunken nights out and opulent dinner parties. Parents plan out their children's lives before they come out of the womb, and great pressure is placed on that child to fulfill that plan. Ask a six-year-old what they want to do for a living, and you're likely to hear them regurgitate what their parents have told them they want to be. How can a child possibly know what they want to do for a living when they've yet to experience life? But that's the way of the world. Many parents have been known to disown their children for choosing a career path different to the one they had been preparing them for their whole life.

Parental and societal pressures are much worse for empaths because they are people pleasers. The empath might become the lawyer their parents expected them to become and suffer terribly because of it. Not only is the job extremely depressing for them because they're constantly exposed to heinous crimes, from the courthouse to the office, but they're forced to deal with many people throughout the day. Then colleagues want to hit the bar after work, and empaths can't say no because they don't want to be judged as unsociable. And then, outside of work, they've got to deal with friends and family.

This extreme overwhelm is too much for empaths to handle, and they often end up finding comfort in addictive behaviors such as drugs and alcohol. When your own mind is working against you, and the only way to escape is through harmful substances, drugs and alcohol will become your numbing agents. The addiction doesn't happen overnight; it starts slowly. You have a drink to find relief from a difficult situation—for example, as well as dealing with constant negative emotions from other people, you've just found out your partner is cheating on you. You live at their place, so you've got to pack up and find somewhere else to live. Your family live too far away for you to stay with them, so you rent an Airbnb for a couple of nights until you can go apartment hunting. You feel depressed, insecure, and lonely. So, to escape the mental torture, you buy a bottle of Jack Daniels, promising to have only one shot. That one shot feels so good, you have another one, and then another until the bottle's empty. You wake up hugging an empty bottle and have the worst hangover, and you promise never to drink excessively again. You lay off it for a couple of weeks, find another apartment and get settled in. You're still upset about the break-up but you're getting over it.

Even though you don't like going to parties, you get an invite from someone at work and decide to go because you're lonely. You get to the party and find that it's really loud, which makes you feel uncomfortable. There are drugs everywhere, and your friend offers you a line of cocaine. You take it without hesitation. And this is the start of your drug and alcohol addiction. In the beginning, you're only using on the weekends, but within a few months, it's every day. You justify your addiction by telling yourself that you've got to cleanse yourself of the toxins from the world. When you're high, you feel great; you're detached from your emotions and the emotions of others, and it genuinely feels as if you've been cleansed— until you wake up in the morning and reality hits you. To escape from your reality, you take more drugs, and thus the cycle begins.

OVERCOMING YOUR ADDICTION

The first step to overcoming addiction is to admit you've got a problem. If you're reading this book, I can only assume you've come to the conclusion that being a dark empath has got something to do with your addiction. Now you've admitted it, you can start looking into getting professional help. Depending on the severity of your addiction, you may be given medication, psychological treatment, or a combination of both. But once you leave the therapist's office, staying clean is your responsibility. Here are some tips on how to do so:

Know Your Triggers: Knowing your triggers is one of the most important factors in beating addiction. A trigger is an internal or external stimulus that entices the former addict to want to use drugs again. For example, anytime you went to the bar with friends, your ritual was to take a couple of hits before you left the house to put you in a state of ecstasy before getting to the bar. The bar becomes a trigger because whenever you go to a bar, you start thinking about using drugs. The way to overcome this is to reject invitations to the bar so the anticipation of going there doesn't lead you to start thinking about drugs.

Cut People Off: If you use drugs with friends, you'll need to cut them off unless they're planning on coming on this journey of sobriety with you. In the majority of instances, that's not the case. There is always one friend who wants to get clean, and one who's not ready yet. As the saying goes, "Misery loves company" —so they'll try and convince you not to quit yet, or to cut down and use on the weekends only. The moment you take the bait and give in, you'll find it even more difficult to quit when you decide to do so for real.

Ask for Help: In general, asking for help is difficult for dark empaths because they're very independent and want everyone to believe their life is a bed of roses. But asking for help becomes even more difficult when it involves admitting you're an addict. Nevertheless, you can't do this alone; you'll need the help of trusted friends and family members to keep you accountable and support you through your recovery.

Find a Support Group: Having the support of friends and family is great, but they've probably never had a personal experience with addiction and don't know what it feels like to walk in your shoes. People in a support group such as AA are all recovering addicts, and you're all going through the same thing.

Find a Hobby: One of the reasons people keep returning to their addictions is boredom. When your mind isn't occupied with doing something constructive, you start hearing your drug or drink of choice calling you. The urge is stronger because you don't have anything else pulling you in another direction. Your mind will eventually convince you to have one more drink, or one more line. But once that buzz hits, you don't stop.

Manage Your Stress: Stress is a natural part of life, but too much stress can become overwhelming. Because dark empaths are so sensitive, the feeling of overwhelm is intensified. When people don't know how to manage stress, they turn to coping mechanisms such as drug and alcohol abuse. Here are some tips to help you deal with stress more effectively:

- **Write Out Your Problems:** When people are dealing with stress, they'll keep thinking about it without coming up with a solution. This is a pointless endeavor, as all it does is make you *more* stressed because the problem is constantly on your mind. However, writing it down gives you the chance to look at your situation for what it is. You can confront it head-on. I would advise that you split the page into three sections, label one side "the problem/problems," label another side "the solution," and label the third side "out of my control." Whatever is out of your control, leave it be, and it will eventually resolve itself. When you come up with a solution, start working on it. What this will do is free your mind from the constraints of the problem, because you are actively working on solving it.

- **Exercise:** One of the most effective ways to relax the mind and the body is to exercise. Exercise improves the mood by releasing endorphins, which are known as "the feel-good hormone." The Centers for Disease Control and Prevention recommend exercising for 150 minutes per week. But if you're new to exercising, you might want to start off by doing light exercises for 15 minutes per day.

- **Deep Breathing:** Deep breathing is a great stress reliever and it will calm you down instantly. You can read more about it in Chapter 11.

- **Muscle Relaxation:** Your muscles tense up when you're stressed, which causes even more stress. Loosening the muscles refreshes the body and relieves tension. You can do this by stretching, having a hot bath, or getting a massage.

- **Focus on Your Hobbies:** Have you neglected your hobbies because you've convinced yourself you don't have time? Research suggests that participating in hobbies is a great stress reliever. Incorporate your hobbies into your day by doing one thing that you enjoy for 30 minutes. It could be doing puzzles, playing golf, knitting, or reading.

- **Get Rid of Your Triggers:** Sometimes we're stressed out because we put ourselves in stressful situations. If you hate your job, spend the week waiting for Friday, spend Sunday dreading Monday, and you're always complaining about how much you can't stand your boss, it might be a good idea to start looking for a new job.

- **Take a Break:** Taking a break can help reset the mind and body so that you can keep going. If you're a goal-oriented person, this might be hard to do if you believe the only way to achieve your goals is to keep going. Taking a break doesn't mean going on vacation—it could mean taking a break from building your side hustle. Instead of working on it every night, do something relaxing like read a book, or watch a movie.

- **Slow Down:** I know you want to reach your goals as soon as possible, but, as mentioned, being on the go all the time is not always the best option. You can become so overwhelmed by what you've got to do that you run around wired on coffee like a speed demon all day. Speed isn't always a good thing, and as the saying goes, "Slow and steady wins the race." Rushing often has the opposite effect; when you rush, you either make mistakes or you miss things and have to go back and redo them. And becoming overwhelmed can lead to burnout. All of these things cause unnecessary stress that you could avoid if you were to slow down.

Look at areas in your life where you could slow down; for example, do you try and answer all your emails in one sitting and then get stressed out because of the number of emails you've got to answer? Break them up so you answer some in the morning, some in the early afternoon, and others late in the afternoon. Or maybe you always drive in the fast lane to get to your destination early and then get frustrated because people aren't driving fast enough? Leave earlier and drive in the slow lane so you can relax on the journey.

- **Eat Properly:** Diet is many people's last priority; cooking is seen as an inconvenience—which is why there are so many fast-food restaurants everywhere. But what people don't understand is that what they put in their body determines how the body operates. A diet of junk food will eventually lead to health problems such as diabetes and heart disease. When the body is forced to work overtime to process all the trash it's fed, that has an effect on the mind. Simple carbohydrates such as processed sugar, soda, and white bread all cause brain fog. When you can't think straight, your stress levels increase.

Don't Give the Addiction Space: I am sorry to be the bearer of bad news, but you will never be fully over your addiction because you will always have cravings. But what happens is your mind becomes strong enough to resist the cravings. Nevertheless, all it takes is for you to give your addiction room in your life, and before you know it, you're using again. This is why there are some people who were sober for ten, fifteen, or twenty years but started using again. It didn't happen suddenly; they had been toying with the idea for a long time before they started using again. They allowed the thought to brew in their mind, and when the going got tough, they thought they'd be able to have one line of cocaine and then leave it alone. But it didn't quite work out like that, and their addiction came back in full force. To prevent this from happening, it's critical that you don't give addiction any space in your life. Here are some tips on how to do this:

- **Self-Talk:** When you feel tempted to go back to your addiction, talk yourself out of it by using reason and logic. Cravings are short-sighted; you get fixated on that one thing and can't see the bigger picture until it's too late. I would advise that you write a list of all the things you stand to lose if you go back to your addiction. Carry it with you at all times, and when the craving hits you, read it out aloud. Unfortunately, most addicts don't see the bigger picture until it's too late. The alcoholic was only concerned about having a drink until he had one too many and killed someone in a DUI accident. Now he's sitting in a jail cell consumed with the agony of the life he's just taken, the life he's about to lose because of how long he'll be in prison, and how his family will suffer because he's not there. You will quickly put things into perspective when you are faced with what you could lose.

- **Don't Dwell on the Past:** There are certain bad memories that can trigger your desire to start using again. It's important that you don't dwell on the past because there's nothing you can do about it. If there is one thing mankind is incapable of, it's turning back the hands of time; you have no control over your past. But you *do* have full control over your future.

- **Reach Out to Someone:** I would suggest having more than one accountability partner during your recovery process so that if one is not there, you can reach out to the other. Have their numbers on speed dial so that when you're craving, you'll have someone to speak to and help you overcome the urge.

- **Surf the Urge:** Urge surfing is a form of mindfulness. It's a technique that focuses on riding out the urge instead of trying to stop it. The idea is that when you focus on trying to stop the urge, it becomes stronger. The technique is called *surfing the urge* because a temptation is similar to a wave. It can come up really strong, but then it settles and goes back down. For this reason, surfers are always looking for the next wave. Urge surfing involves acknowledging the craving when it comes and accepting it for what it is. If you're alone, sit down, close your eyes, and focus on the thoughts and feelings going through your body. Speak them out loud and name exactly what you are thinking and how you are feeling. For example, you might be thinking, "I would feel so good if I could have one line of cocaine right now. Just one line and I would throw the rest away. My heart is beating really fast, and my legs are shaking." Keep describing these thoughts and feelings until they are no longer there.

- **Cognitive Behavioral Therapy (CBT):** Cognitive behavioral therapy is a psychological technique that helps you change the way you think and behave. It is based on the idea that your thoughts and feelings are connected to your actions, which means that negative thinking is connected to negative actions. Cognitive behavioral therapy uses a variety of approaches to help with cravings, including visualization, distraction, and redirection. When the craving comes, distract yourself or think about something else until the craving has settled.

  Visualization puts you into a relaxed state as you imagine being in a peaceful setting. Cognitive behavioral therapy can also help you recognize cognitive distortions. During a drug craving, a cognitive distortion is called *catastrophizing*, which is thinking about the worst-case scenario. You'll think things like, "The only thing that will make this craving go away is if I give in to the craving," or, "I can't do this; I'll always be an addict." Cognitive behavioral therapy teaches you how to examine your thoughts objectively, which enables you to come to a rational conclusion.

I knew James was a true empath when he kept getting the same illnesses and pain in his body as me. If we spent time around someone with back pain, the next day we would both have back pain in the exact same places. It was the strangest thing, but evidence suggested that there was more to his disturbing behavior than him just being an asshole. In the next chapter, you'll learn all about emphatic illnesses and pain.

CHAPTER 15:

EMPATHIC ILLNESSES AND PAIN

s your partner always sick? Have they been to the doctor's and been told there is nothing wrong with them? Or have they been given medication that doesn't alleviate all the symptoms of an illness? If you've answered yes to any of these questions, your partner is most likely dealing with empathic illness and pain. Judy Orloff, author of *The Empath's Survival Guide*, refers to people like this as "physical empaths." Their bodies are so porous that when they're around sick people, they absorb their symptoms. Additionally, they are susceptible to certain conditions such as migraines, muscle pain, and joint pain because of the continuous flow of energy they absorb. The only way to deal with it is to learn how to protect yourself against empathic illnesses and pain. Here are some tips:

Maintain Your Boundaries: In Chapter 2, I discussed how to set healthy boundaries, and it's extremely important that you maintain these to protect yourself against empathic illnesses. One of the interesting contradictions about being a dark empath is that they go through the same struggles as a normal empath, but their dark side causes them to inflict the same pain on people. Not only do dark empaths attract people who constantly violate their boundaries, they also struggle to maintain them. Dark empaths have a strong desire to help others in need—it's such a natural urge that running to the aid of an upset friend or family member happens automatically. Additionally, because these friends and family members are so used to the support they get, they expect it, and when you're not there, it's a problem. This is especially true of manipulative and narcissistic people. They will make you feel extremely guilty for not coming to their rescue. But what they fail to understand is that, although they feel better when they release their hurt and pain, dark empaths take on their burden. So, before you go rushing off to the next 911 emergency call from someone in need, determine whether you're mentally and spiritually strong enough to deal with their problems at that time. If not, say no. It's important to understand that, even though you'll feel bad for not being there, you'll feel worse when you go and deal with a situation you're not equipped to handle.

One of the many negative characteristics of dark empaths is they will play the savior role and then complain that they've too much on their plate, and complain even more when they get sick. Unfortunately, some of your wounds are self-inflicted, and as you learn to create healthy boundaries and stick to them, not only will your physical and mental state improve, you'll also repel toxic people. Toxic people hate it when they're not in control and will quickly move on to the next victim when they realize you're not as weak as they thought you were.

Practice Detachment: Detachment means not getting emotionally involved in every situation that you're exposed to. Being empathic is only beneficial when it doesn't take over your life. Dark empaths often find themselves in a state of distress over other people's problems because they feel so deeply. However, for the sake of your mental and physical health, you can't afford to do this all the time. It's important to understand that detachment isn't about becoming cold and aloof; it's about understanding that you can't fix everyone. Feeling another person's pain isn't the problem, but thinking you're responsible for healing their pain *is*. An unfortunate fact of life is that pain is a part of the growth process. If people are unable to successfully navigate the trials of life, they will never become who they were supposed to be. Compare this to the butterfly analogy. The caterpillar doesn't like being in the cocoon; it's dark and lonely in there, and he wants to get out as soon as possible. When the transformation takes place and he starts breaking out of his shell as a butterfly, he struggles to get out because the process hurts and he can't wait to emerge with his new wings. But if another caterpillar sees his struggle and helps him break out of the cocoon, his wings won't develop properly and he'll have difficulty flying. That's what dark empaths do when they step in and fix everything because they feel they need to—sometimes it does more harm than good.

When you understand that the struggle is a critical lesson in the school of life, your desire to become the handyman in every situation will decrease. Additionally, there are some people who don't *want* healing; they're comfortable in their pain and misery. You can give them the exact solution they need to solve their problems, but they'll never take action. In fact, they'll find a problem for every solution you give them. You'll waste your time and energy trying to fix someone who doesn't want to be fixed.

Practice Journaling: Dark empaths don't have the liberty of having someone else's shoulder to cry on. Because they're always the go-to person when other people are in need, the assumption is that they're strong and they've got it all together. As a result, dark empaths are known to suffer in silence. They internalize their emotions—and that's one of the reasons they get sick. A powerful way to release emotions is through journaling. When the way you feel is released onto paper, its power is reduced because it's no longer eating away at your soul. You can look at it and see it for what it is. Anytime you have painful or negative emotional experiences, write them down. Before putting pen to paper, ground yourself, then start writing. You'll feel emotional during the writing process, but that's fine. Cry if you need to; it's all part of expressing your feelings and releasing the emotions that can harm you if they stay bottled up.

After you've got everything out of your system, write out this statement: "Thank you for helping release negative harmful energy due to what I've experienced. These emotions have no power over me. I am now free to continue living a happy, healthy, and productive life." Once you're done, close the journal and see it as symbolic of closing the door on something that has distressed you. Separate yourself from any energy attached to it. Some dark empaths feel that they get more closure when they rip the pages out and burn them. Get into the habit of journaling anytime you go through a negative experience.

Submerge Yourself in Water: Water is exceptionally helpful when it comes to ridding yourself of negative energy because it invigorates you, surrounds you with liquid light, and fills you with positive energy. There are several different techniques you can use, including the following:

- **Epsom Salt Bath:** Epsom salt is a well-known energy cleanser. Add two cups to a bath, and a few drops of an essential oil such as lavender or orange, and soak in it until you feel better. When you pull the plug out, watch the water flow down the drain and envision all the negative energy that was attached to you being washed away.

- **Take a Shower:** As the water runs down your body, envision all the negative energy attached to you washing away and disappearing away forever down the drain.

- **Swim Outdoors:** If you live in a warm climate, or it's during the summer months, go for a swim in the sea. Swimming makes you feel free and relaxed. When you get out of the sea, you leave any negative energy that was attached to you behind.

AVOID THE THINGS THAT DON'T MAKE YOU FEEL GOOD

Avoiding the things that don't make you feel good is about learning to say *no*. And when you do say *no*, don't shy away from telling people why. But be prepared for the backlash—they'll attempt to shame you into participating by saying things like, "Well, the more you expose yourself to the things you're uncomfortable around, the easier it will be for you." This is not how it works; by exposing yourself to toxic environments, you'll become *more* sensitive to them. Think about it like this: why are we told not to expose ourselves to radiation? Because it's dangerous and can cause conditions such as cancer and tumors. These conditions don't manifest immediately; it takes constant exposure to the radiation. The same is true about toxic environments. You know what's not good for you, so instead of giving in to the need to people-please, don't put yourself in these situations.

Saying *no* will quickly weed out the people who are not for you. Your true friends will understand how important it is to protect your energy. If you're sensitive to noise and lights and they want to go to a rock concert, arrange to meet them at a quiet restaurant afterwards. You can sit down over a meal and they can tell you all about the concert. It will benefit you much more if you hear about it instead of being a part of it.

Maybe you don't like being in an open-plan office at work because you're exposed to everyone and everything. As a result, your entire day from start to finish is one big anxiety fest. You wake up anxious because you don't want to go into work, then you go into work anxious because you don't want to deal with being in an open-plan space. And you go to bed anxious thinking about the hell you're going to go through the next day. In a situation like this, be bold enough to ask your manager if you can move into a side office. If your manager doesn't empathize with your situation, or there are no side offices, you might consider getting a job that can accommodate your needs.

If you know that certain toxic people (even family) who make you feel ill when you're around them are going to be at a social gathering, don't go. Think about it like this: if you knew you were allergic to crabs and they made you break out into a rash, and you were served crab at a dinner party, would you eat it just to appease the host? No. You would eat everything else and leave the crab. So, if you're sensitive to spiritual energy, and being around certain people makes you feel sick, avoid them like the plague—and don't feel guilty about it either.

Nevertheless, if you feel you've reached a point where you're strong enough to fend off negative energy, and you know how to prepare for these situations, that's fine. But if you know you're not ready yet, stay away.

Anti-Inflammatory Diet: I don't subscribe to the "one size fits all" theology when it comes to diet because everyone is different. Some people have experienced tremendous health benefits from a plant-based diet, while others have not. The same is true of every diet. So, before changing your diet, book an appointment with an allergist or a naturopath to help you determine which foods are helpful and which are harmful to you. A lot of dark empaths, however, do find an anti-inflammatory diet extremely helpful, especially those suffering from autoimmune disorders. An anti-inflammatory diet eliminates foods such as white carbohydrates, sugar, and red meat while incorporating more whole grains, fruits, and vegetables. Some dark empaths have had great success on a vegan diet; others prefer the keto or paleo diet. With trial and error, you'll find the foods that nourish your body and make you feel vibrant and healthy. As a result, you'll reduce your chances of becoming physically and mentally ill.

Protect Your Energy: Protecting your energy by creating an energy barrier is perhaps one of the most effective methods for warding off bad vibes when you're in a social setting. However, it takes a lot of practice to perfect, so be mindful of this and be patient with yourself when you get started. There are two ways to create an energy barrier: with white light, and by summoning your spirit guides:

- **White Light:** Before going out in public or dealing with toxic people, envision a white light that radiates a few feet away from you. You will feel as if you're in a cocoon. The space between you and the white light is where the energy flows. Imagine a small hole at the top and the bottom of the cocoon. This allows the light from above to flow down onto you, and the negative energy to flow out from you through the bottom hole. Once you feel as if you're fully protected, leave the house in your cocoon.

- **Spirit Guide:** Your spirit guides can be angels, devas, a dead relative or any other positive energy being you know. Before leaving the house, summon them to accompany you on your journey. Envision them standing in front of you, taking all the negative energy on your behalf. Your spirit guide is like a bodyguard, and when you walk with them, no harm can come to you.

- **Become More Aware of Your Body:** It's not uncommon for empaths to feel completely detached from the human experience. Because you constantly feel overwhelmed, you've trained yourself since childhood to filter out the noise. As a coping mechanism, you escape into another world. The problem with this type of escapism is that it's not a conscious act. Therefore, you leave yourself vulnerable to negative energy. It's similar to going out and leaving your front door unlocked. It may be more convenient for you when you return because you won't need to use your key to open the door—but a thief could easily walk into your house and steal your valuables.

Being more present will be uncomfortable when you first get started because you're not used to experiencing every part of your being. But it will get easier once you start using energy barriers and enforcing healthy boundaries. You won't need to escape anymore because you'll be fully protected. You will no longer feel imprisoned in your body; instead, it will become a protective fortress. Tai Chi and Vinyasa flow yoga are great ways to become more aware of your body. Here are some yoga exercises you can practice to get started:

The Plank Pose

- Lie on your stomach and push yourself up with your hands and feet so you are in a press-up position. Your body should be perfectly aligned with the floor.

- Your hips and shoulders should be in line and your shoulders on top of your wrists.

- Lengthen your body by stretching through your heels and the crown of your head.

- Hold this pose for 60 seconds.

Tip: Keep your elbows unlocked, and don't sink your hips into the floor or push them up too high towards the ceiling.

Dog Facing Down Pose

- Lie on your stomach and take a deep breath in. As you exhale, take a deep breath out and push your entire body up off the floor so your body makes the shape of a triangle. You should feel the blood rush to your head.

- Keep your hands and feet shoulder-width apart.

- Keep your spine extended, your heels pressed into the mat, and your buttocks pushed up towards the ceiling.

- Hold this pose for 60 seconds.

Tip: Sink your heels into the floor and keep your toes pointed towards the front of the mat.

Dog Facing Upward Pose

- Lie on your stomach with your legs stretched out behind you.

- Take a deep breath inwards and lift your body up off the mat with your hands.

- Push yourself as high up as you can go and lock your elbows.

- The top part of your thighs should also be lifted off the mat.

- Hold this pose for 60 seconds.

Tip: As you position your hips towards the floor, open your chest in an upwards position.

The Cobra Pose

- Lie on your stomach and use your back to lift your chest off the ground.

- Keep your arms bent and remain in a low pose.

- Keep all your weight in the tops of your feet and your pelvis, not your hands.

- Hold this pose for 60 seconds.

Tip: Keep your legs and pelvis fixed to the floor while you lift your chest.

Keep Your Lymphatic System Healthy: The lymphatic system and the immune system are closely related; therefore, you'll need to make sure the lymphatic system is in good working order. As well as consuming a good diet and doing yoga, it's also advised that you go for a lymph-drainage massage once every three months. A massage therapist will use slight pressure and essential oils to stimulate your lymph nodes. The massage will drain the stored swelling caused by illness, which will boost your immune system.

Weight gain is a unique struggle amongst empaths, and it left me broken for many years because I couldn't overcome it. When I realized James struggled with it too, I was even more convinced that dark empaths are empaths in disguise. You can read all about it in Chapter 16.

CHAPTER 16:

DARK EMPATHS AND WEIGHT GAIN

D ark empaths don't like talking about weight because it makes them feel extremely uncomfortable. They either want to gain weight or lose it; the happy medium is almost nonexistent. In fact, dark empaths are known for not keeping weighing scales in their homes. Dark empath or not, humans in general don't appreciate how truly awesome the body is. It detoxifies itself, heals itself, repairs, and destroys unwanted cells. But because the media places such emphasis on the way we look, we are more focused on the appearance of the body rather than how it actually works. We go on extreme diets to starve ourselves, and gorge on food to gain weight. We have plastic surgery to change the shape of our noses, lips, and anything else we don't like about ourselves. When the body appears to be working the way it should, we take it for granted. But as soon as it breaks down, we start complaining and forget that we've spent the majority of our lives abusing it.

As harsh as it may sound, when dark empaths neglect their gift, they're abusing their bodies. Of course, some empaths neglect their gift in ignorance because they don't know they're empaths. Then there are others who don't know how to nurture their gift, and others who know what they need to do but don't do it because it requires discipline and dedication. To avoid gaining weight, there are certain strategies the dark empath must implement (I'll discuss them at the end of the chapter). But first, let's take a look at some of the main reasons they gain weight.

HORMONAL IMBALANCES, AUTOIMMUNE DISORDERS, AND ALLERGIES

Dark empaths tend to suffer from hormonal imbalances, autoimmune disorders, neurological issues, and allergies. According to medical experts, being in a constant state of overwhelm due to emotions, environmental stresses, toxins, and sensations causes the immune system to overwork, which eventually leads to it shutting down. Autoimmune disorders are linked to diet, but some healthy foods can also cause weight gain. For example, celiac disease causes weight gain due to the gluten in grains such as spelt, barley, rye, and wheat. Allergies and conditions such as polycystic ovarian syndrome (PCOS) cause the body to have inflammatory reactions to certain foods, and to hold water. If you find that you keep gaining weight despite consuming a healthy diet, you might think about working with a naturopathic doctor to get to the root of the problem.

BODY DYSMORPHIC DISORDER

Because dark empaths take on the problems of so many people, they feel alienated from their bodies—almost as if they don't own their body, and they're renting it out to the world. They see themselves as purely energetic beings; their physical shells don't matter. Therefore, they see their bodies as cages that are either too soft, too hard, too tight, too big, or anything other than who they truly are. Even if they are of normal weight, they'll convince themselves they're either too thin or too fat and become obsessed with achieving the perfect weight. So if they think they're too thin, they'll keep eating in the hopes of gaining weight. But because their reality is warped, they'll end up overweight because they don't know when to stop.

Comfort Eating

As mentioned, some dark empaths suffer from crippling anxiety and depression because they get stuck with everyone else's negative energy, and they don't know how to rid it from their bodies. One of the ways they soothe themselves is by comfort eating. Comfort eating involves consuming high-fat, sweet, and fatty foods such as french fries, cookies, ice cream, and fried chicken. Because dark empaths are continuously overwhelmed, they comfort-eat all the time, which leads to weight gain.

A Form of Self-Defense

While some people relish the attention they get from the opposite sex, dark empaths hate it. Because they are so sensitive and can feel everything around them, when dark empaths are ogled, it makes them feel extremely uncomfortable. If they have experienced sexual abuse or trauma, they will find the attention even more upsetting. As a result, their minds and bodies work to protect them from predators—and they achieve this by gaining weight. Because the dark empath feels unattractive when they're overweight, they'll overeat intentionally to pile on the pounds. When a person feels unattractive, that energy is received by others, which acts as a repellent to the opposite sex.

Natural Protection

In a mosh pit at a rock concert, hundreds of people are crowded into one space, thrashing and bouncing around while ear-splitting music plays. Afterwards, the body feels as if it's been tossed around like a ragdoll. Whereas the average person might go to a rock concert once and have this experience every couple of years, the dark empath feels this way the majority of the time. Traveling on public transport, for example, can feel like a mosh pit because so many people are getting on and off. Not only do dark empaths feel emotions internally, they are also felt in the nerves, muscles, and bones. It's a terrible ordeal, and those with a smaller frame are even more sensitive to energy waves. Therefore, some dark empaths will intentionally put on weight to protect themselves. Compare it to wrapping yourself up in a warm duvet in a cold house; you only feel cold once the duvet is removed.

How Dark Empaths Can Avoid Weight Gain

As mentioned, some dark empaths intentionally put on weight as a defense mechanism or a form of protection. Although this may seem logical, it is harmful. Overweight people are prone to many health conditions, such as diabetes, heart disease, and gall bladder disease. Therefore, it's important that you get your weight issues under control.

See a Doctor: Your first step should be to see a doctor for an accurate diagnosis of any health conditions you may have that are contributing to your weight gain. If you've got any underlying issues, your main focus should be on getting them under control. Your healing may require changing your diet to ensure you're getting the right nutrients to fuel your body.

Confront Your Emotions: Holding on to negative emotions cause several health problems, and weight gain is one of them. Many of these trapped negative emotions don't even belong to you, making your problems even more difficult to resolve. You can confront your emotions and release trapped emotions by doing the following:

- **Acknowledge Your Feelings:** Become so submerged in your emotional world that you are fully aware of your feelings and capable of digesting them in healthy ways. Start by understanding and connecting with your emotions. You might find it difficult to identify and put a label on your emotions because they've been repressed for so long. It's important to label your emotions, because studies have proven that doing so decreases their intensity. However, if you find it difficult to acknowledge your feelings, you may need to see a mental health professional.

- **Confront Your Trauma:** Some trapped emotions are due to unresolved childhood trauma. This might include:
  - Sexual, physical, mental, and/or emotional abuse
  - The death of a loved one
  - Bullying
  - Neglect
  - Parental separation
  - Household dysfunction

  Additionally, unresolved childhood trauma can manifest in several ways, including:
  - Depression
  - Social withdrawal
  - Self-blame
  - Blaming others

  According to psychologist David Olson, it's important to grieve the fact that you didn't get what you needed at the time in order to heal. Once you've come to terms with the grief, identify the strategy you've used as a coping mechanism. For example, if your parents made you feel like a burden as a child, your coping mechanism might be independence, which means you never ask for help when you need it.

- **Movement:** Somatic experiencing uses a "body first" approach to deal with unprocessed emotions and trauma in the body. The idea is to release those emotions through movement. Movement can include:
  - Stretching
  - Dance
  - Yoga
  - Abdominal breathing
  - Meditative walking
  - Tai chi
  - Qi gong
  - Martial arts
  - Shaking

  Moving the body in this way encourages the release of trapped emotions, while training the brain to recognize the difference between relaxation and tension.

- **Practice Stillness:** We are most present when we are still because we are better able to tap into our thoughts and feelings. Scientists refer to this time during which the brain is in a state of idleness as the its *default mode network*. This is typically when people start daydreaming. We live in a world where busyness is valued over stillness. We are always on the go, and if we're not, we're accused of being too chilled out. There are several ways to practice stillness, including:
  - Meditation
  - Sitting in nature
  - Breathing exercises

- Progressive muscle relaxation
- Listening to relaxing music

- **Shadow Work:** Even if all you remember about growing up is happiness, everyone experiences childhood trauma. During the infant years, the human psyche is so fragile that the most seemingly insignificant things can cause damage. For example, perhaps your mother told you to stop crying or to calm down when you were upset about something. She may have been saying it in the sweetest, softest voice, but what it did was invalidate your feelings. Even though your mother was being nice in trying to settle you, psychologically you weren't ready to settle down. You wanted to keep crying until you didn't feel sad anymore. You subconsciously internalized this incident and interpreted it to mean that you need to keep your emotions to yourself, or that they're something to be ashamed of. As a result, you feel there are some parts of you that are unacceptable, and you hide them.

  Shadow work involves engaging with your unconscious mind to discover the parts of yourself that you hide and repress. The shadow is the hidden part yourself you spend a lot of time and energy trying to avoid. Here are some tips on how to practice shadow work:

- **Locate Your Inner Shadow:** Your shadow is often hidden in your bad habits. You think you've buried these parts of yourself, but they're a major part of your life because they hold you back. One way, therefore, of locating your inner shadow is to pay attention to your bad habits.

  Another way to locate your inner shadow is through your triggers. Consciously, you might not remember the trauma, but your subconscious mind responds to certain triggers. You'll know when something is a trigger because the way you react to it is out of proportion to the trigger. For example, you might get really angry when you hear anyone saying the words *calm down*. When you hear it being said to someone else, you get angry, but when it's said to *you*, you lash out at the person.

Lastly, you can find your inner shadow by paying attention to the things you project onto others. For example, it might agitate you to see people get excited over what appear to you as small things. So, you burst their bubble by telling the person to calm down. You do this because you weren't allowed to get excited over small things as a child and you were shut down because of it. Now you grow annoyed when you see other people getting excited over small things, because your inner child doesn't think it's fair that others should get to celebrate small things when you couldn't.

- **Go Back to Your Childhood:** If your parents are ready to have this conversation, it would help to speak to them. Unfortunately, some parents are not willing to accept that they played a role in traumatizing their children. As far as they're concerned, they did the best they could with what they had. If this sounds like your parents, think back to times in your childhood when you were treated as less than or demonized for your bad behavior. Were you punished for emotions such as sadness or anger? If so, you may repress these emotions in adulthood and try to appear happy all the time because you don't want to upset anyone.

- **Don't Shame Your Shadow:** Avoid shaming or feeling ashamed of your shadow because it's a part of you, and that's who you are. It's difficult enough feeling as if you are not accepted by others, but when you don't feel accepted by *yourself*, it's even harder. You can't control how other people feel about you, but you *can* control how you feel about yourself. Be kind to yourself and have compassion for your shadow.

- **Journal:** Writing about your shadow will further help you to accept it. Your shadow is those dark, depressing thoughts you have about yourself. Write your thoughts down without overthinking—just let it all flow out onto the paper. You'll feel very uncomfortable doing this, but this is your shadow's way of feeling heard and seen by you. When you're done, read back what you've written. Do this every day for thirty days, and you'll notice a pattern. There will be some things you repeat. These are the things you need to pay attention to.

- **Express Yourself:** Whatever way you feel most comfortable expressing your inner shadow, do it. This might be through art, singing or dancing. During the creative process, allow yourself to feel every emotion.

- **Have a Conversation:** Have a conversation with your inner shadow by asking yourself questions and giving yourself an honest answer. This is not an out-loud conversation; it is done through meditation. You will hear the conversation in your inner being.

SHADOW WORK PROMPTS

Here are some shadow work prompts to help start your healing journey:

- What negative emotions do you try to avoid and why?

- How do you spend your time when you're bored? What alleviates the boredom?

- What does failure look like to you? When was the last time you failed at something, and how did it make you feel? Does failure scare you? If so, why?

- When do you not show yourself compassion and why?

- Growing up, what were your parents' core values?

- What are your core values and what makes them important to you?

- What are the differences between your and your parents' core values? What made you change them?

- What trait do you not have that you envy in others? Why don't you have this trait?

- When/who makes you feel the most valued?

- Who has disappointed you the most in your life?

- Are you holding a grudge against anyone? If so, why can't you let it go?

- When do you feel unsafe?

- When do you feel self-conscious?

- How do you feel when in the presence of drama?

- Do your parents have character traits you admire?

- Do your parents have character traits you don't like?

- What is your worst character trait?

- What's your worst childhood memory?

- What lies do you tell yourself?

- What hidden part of you do you wish people understood?

- Which friends do you feel the most secure around?

- Which friends make you feel uncomfortable?

- Do you remember the last time you self-sabotaged? Why did you do it, and what was the trigger?

- What emotions reveal your bad side and why?

- What are you most afraid of? Do you think you'll ever be ready to expose yourself to this fear?

- Who has hurt you the most? Write them a letter and tell them why. (Don't send it.)

- What incidents in your life do you regret?

- Who makes you feel envious and why?

- For what reasons do you judge others?

- What are the worst traits a person can have?

- How do you think people perceive you? How would you describe yourself to others?

Appreciate Your Body: Appreciating your body is extremely difficult. It's in the body where we feel all the pain and anguish, which is why it can be so hard to appreciate it. This situation is a double-edged sword because the more disdain you have for your body, the less likely you are to treat it with the kindness it needs in order to thrive. I put "Appreciate Your Body" at the end of this chapter because it will become easier after you've been diagnosed with any health conditions and have confronted your emotions. One of the most effective ways to learn how to appreciate your body is by conditioning your mind through affirmations. When you first get started, repeating affirmations will feel very uncomfortable because you are so used to negative self-talk. But in the same way you've conditioned yourself to believe you're unworthy through negative self-talk, you can condition yourself you're worthy through *positive* self-talk. Here are some powerful affirmations to repeat to yourself—I recommend looking in the mirror and saying them every morning and every evening:

- My body is a powerful vessel for the greater good.

- I nourish and fuel my body with the right foods.

- I am grateful for the body I have.

- My body is full of energy and life.

- Because I care for and love my body, my body cares for and loves me.

- My body is surrounded with healing energy.

- I feel good when I take care of my body.

- I treat my body well because it is my greatest gift.

- My body is a pillar of strength.

- I am complete, perfect, and whole just the way I am.

Do you want to know why your dark empath partner seems so heartless? Find out in the next chapter.

CHAPTER 17:

WHEN EMPATHY TURNS INTO APATHY

Compassion fatigue is a condition that affects workers such as nurses, caregivers, and those who work in animal shelters, who witness the suffering of people and animals. They feel so much empathy and compassion that, over time, they become shell-shocked and overwhelmed by it, and this causes them to suppress their emotions. When a person suppresses their emotions for too long, they stop feeling them, which leads to apathy. Apathy is also experienced by dark empaths because they are so connected to the emotions of others. Dark empaths who don't understand their gift become overwhelmed, and so numbing their emotions becomes their coping mechanism.

Dark empaths become inwardly aware and hypersensitive, erecting a protective shield to block out the constant flow of negative emotions they feel from others. Many feel they don't have a choice; it's either live an exhausted life, or protect themselves at all costs. The problem is that a protective shield doesn't just protect you against the emotions of others, it also protects you from your own emotions. As a result, you risk becoming so coldhearted that nothing affects you anymore. A close loved one could die and you'd go back to watching your movie as if nothing had happened. Becoming emotionally numb is just as bad as being overly emotional; they both have negative consequences. Despite how much safer it feels to no longer be the victim of everyone else's emotions, you're doing yourself more harm than good.

Apathy deprives you of the joys and wonders that add substance and vitality to life. Whether it was reading, bike riding, or going to the movies, the things you once enjoyed doing will become mundane and meaningless. You won't have the motivation to do anything and will spend most of the time in whatever safe haven you've erected for yourself. Apathy also makes you indifferent to the feelings of your closest friends and relatives. This can cause tension in your relationships because where you were once emotionally invested in them, you have grown indifferent, and it could come across as if you don't care. Apathy is even more detrimental if you have a spouse. You'll find yourself getting agitated and frustrated when they've got genuine issues and they need your support. You'll start seeing them as emotionally needy and will withdraw from them. The problem becomes even worse when you've got kids. Instead of the lovable creatures they are, they'll become annoying attention seekers whom you can't be bothered to deal with. Eventually, you'll live life going through the motions and only cherishing the moments when you don't have to deal with anyone.

HOW TO PREVENT APATHY

Preventing apathy requires living a balanced life, but living a balanced life is difficult to achieve. It's all about finding that middle ground so you're not completely worn out by others' emotions, and nor are you completely shielding yourself from emotions. So you'll need to do some self-evaluating to discover your tipping point so you can protect yourself accordingly. Here's how:

Know What Drains You: Pay attention to the things and people that are the most draining. Do certain friends and family members deplete your energy? Limit the amount of time you spend with them, or, as harsh as it sounds, cut them off altogether. Does going to the mall set you off on an emotional frenzy? Stop going, or go when you know you're strong enough to handle it.

Create a Safe Space: A safe space is somewhere in your home you can go to and calm down when you're feeling overwhelmed. Here are some tips on how to create a safe space:

- **Choose a Room:** Whether it's your bedroom or the office, choose somewhere in your home to use as a dedicated safe space. If you live with other people, tell them about your safe space so they understand your needs. Let them know that when the "do not disturb" sign is up, they shouldn't come into the room.

- **Decorate It:** Because it's a place for you to unwind, it should be decorated accordingly. Start by giving it a good clean so it's free from any clutter, and then decorate it in a way that's therapeutic to you and will aid relaxation. Paint the room in a muted tone such as gray, green, or blue. These colors trigger feelings of emotional safety and well-being. Get your senses involved by using essential oils, incense, or candles. Scents like rose, lavender, and bergamot are known for their relaxation and stress-relieving qualities. Add a comfy chair, some pillows and blankets so you can sit and read, meditate, or do some breathing exercises.

- **During Your Quiet Time:** Don't bring any gadgets into the room with you such as a phone, laptop or iPad. The idea is to completely unplug from everything. If you want music, use an MP3 player so your phone doesn't become a distraction.

Create a Shield: A shield protects you against negative energy. Think about it like a healthy immune system; it's always working, but when harmful bacteria comes along, it acts accordingly. As mentioned, apathy happens when this shield is up all the time. This is similar to an autoimmune response that attacks healthy, normal cells in the body. It's not that there's anything wrong with feeling the emotions of others; it's natural to feel happy or sad when someone else is feeling these emotions. The problems start when you absorb emotions such as despair, hate, or anger when they're not coming from you. Here are a few shielding techniques to use when you're in a high-energy environment:

Crystals: Crystals make the perfect shield for empaths because they absorb negative energy. You can wear them as jewelry, or carry one with you when you go out and hold it in the palm of your hand when you start feeling an energy shift. You can also place them by your bed to help get rid of negative energy you've picked up throughout the day. You'll need to clean your crystals every once in a while or they'll lose their abilities and become stagnant. You can do this by running them under water (check beforehand that they're not the type of crystals that dissolve in water), or you can recharge them with the moon by putting them outside overnight. Here are some of the best crystals for shielding:

- **Pyrite:** You will also hear pyrite referred to as fool's gold. It helps calm the mind and body.

- **Clear Quartz:** Clear quartz is similar to the amethyst crystal. It will repel negative energy and bring positive energy into an environment.

- **Smithsonite:** After a difficult day, smithsonite helps people relax and maintain calmness.

- **Black Tourmaline:** Black tourmaline is a popular crystal amongst empaths because of its electromagnetic frequency absorption capabilities. This is one crystal that people like carrying with them at all times and will typically wear around the neck as a talisman.

- **Black Jade:** To increase your intuition so you're aware when negative energy is on its way, carry a black jade crystal wherever you go. It helps you have a deeper connection with your intuition.

- Obsidian: This stone is renowned for its protective energy. It helps restore a damaged aura and further protects it against incoming negative energy.

- **Citrine:** This crystal has been compared to the sun and is known to increase confidence, balance emotions, and ward off negative energy.

- **Amethyst:** This astonishing purple crystal will push negative energy out and bring positive energy in. It's also good for enhancing your psychic abilities, which will further protect you against psychological attacks.

Visualization: Visualization helps protect you from your external environment. If you haven't done it before, you'll need to practice before you start using the technique because it takes extreme focus for it to be effective. Follow these steps for effective visualization:

- With your eyes closed, imagine being surrounded by a bright white light.

- Imagine the white light getting brighter and more intense as it penetrates your mind and muscles.

- Imagine it penetrating all the dark places in your body and mind.

- Keep visualizing this until you start feeling lighter, and then open your eyes.

- To enhance the feeling, use the mantra, "I am the light."

Relaxation: When the body is in a relaxed state, all pent-up negative energy is released. Relaxation involves getting in touch with your body. The next step is conscious breathing, and then the relaxing of the muscles. The more relaxed you become, the more negative energy is released. It helps to use essential oils such as lavender, sweet orange, bergamot, and patchouli to get deeper into your relaxation. Here are the steps you will need to follow to get into a relaxed state:

- Sit or lie in a comfortable position.

- Pay attention to your body and the areas where you feel tension.

- Start taking slow, deep breaths, and exhale into the tense areas of your body.

- Start tensing your muscles from your head down to your toes.

- Repeat these steps until you've got yourself into a relaxed state.

Veiling: If you've ever attended a Kundalini Yoga class, you'll notice a lot of students wearing a white turban or scarf tied around their heads. According to Yogi Bhajan, a prominent figure in Kundalini Yoga, wearing a head covering during practice helps protect your energy, enhance your thoughts and create a stronger focus on your third eye. Bhajan also recommends wearing white because it adds an extra foot to your aura, which provides additional protection against negative energy. It also ensures that you radiate positive energy, which helps inspire and motivate the people you come into contact with. So, if you feel you need an extra layer of protection when leaving the house, wear a white head covering.

Smudging: White sage is an herb renowned for its cleansing properties. You can either purchase it as leaves or incense sticks. For best results, open the window and leave the herb to burn. The smoke absorbs the negative energy, and it's blown out of the window.

A Protection Jar: Find a glass jar and fill it up with items containing protective properties such as spices, herbs, sigils, symbols, gems, stones, and crystals. Whilst in a meditative state, charge the jar with your intentions. You can make several of these jars and keep one on your desk at work, and the others in your car and the rooms in your home.

Grounding: With all the negative energy dark empaths attract, and the many ups and downs they experience in life, it's difficult to remain grounded. Grounding involves using nature to assist you in feeling calm and relaxed. Many cultures worship Mother Earth because of her life-giving properties; when you ground yourself using Mother Earth, she infuses you with her light. Follow these steps to ground yourself:

- Go outside and find a secluded grassy area.

- Remove your shoes and socks and feel the earth connecting with your feet.

- Close your eyes and start taking slow, deep breaths.

- Once you get into a relaxed state, imagine the negative energy you are carrying as it travels down through your body and into the earth.

- Absorb the calming effect of the earth underneath your feet, and imagine it filling you up with all its goodness.

Self-Reflection: The most powerful form of energetic protection is love. We can get plenty of love from outside sources such as our parents, siblings, lovers, and animals. However, the highest form of love is loving oneself. Unfortunately, most people do not know how to love themselves and rely on receiving this from others. Like attracts like, and one of the reasons some dark empaths pick up on so much negative energy is that they're carrying around unresolved trauma, which makes it difficult for them to love themselves. Therefore, healing is the first step in self-reflection. This may require seeing a therapist, but you can start by doing the following:

- Confront your fears by writing them down. Think about everything you're afraid of and the reasons you're afraid of these things.

- Determine whether your fears are rational or a figment of your imagination.

- Create an action plan to start working on your fears. For example, if you're afraid of public speaking, start looking for speaking engagements.

- The more you challenge your fears, the healthier your self-esteem will become.

- Practice self-love by writing down three things you love about yourself.

- Look in the mirror and say, "I love you."

How to Overcome Apathy

If you're currently struggling with apathy, you can overcome it by re-engaging with life. Right now, I'm sure the last thing you want to do is get out there and start mingling again; you'd rather stay in your safe haven and let everyone else get on with it. But if your empath gift is going to be put to good use, overcoming your apathy is a must. Here are some tips on how to do this:

- **Get a New Hobby:** When you're fed up with life, nothing interests you anymore. The things you used to love no longer appeal to you, and, as I've said several times throughout this chapter, you'd rather curl up in a ball under your duvet than deal with the world. However, getting a new hobby can help break that cycle and give you something to look forward to again. As mentioned, it won't be easy, but you can start by choosing a hobby online to avoid the socializing aspect of it.

- **Get Moving:** Apathy causes mental and physical lethargy; you simply can't be bothered to do anything. The end goal should be to start exercising daily, but you can start by simply moving your body. Whether it's dancing, walking, yoga, or playing tag with your kids, moving will enhance your sense of well-being. This in turn will relax your body, increase your energy, and improve your sleep. The more your body is energized through movement, the more motivation you'll have to incorporate exercise into your daily routine.

- **Celebrate Your Wins:** Pat yourself on the back for every small win. By celebrating your wins, you'll start focusing on the things you *can* do instead of the things you *can't*. If you've been leaving your plates to pile up in the kitchen sink because you've had no motivation, a win could be washing the dishes. Whatever it is, celebrate by treating yourself to something small. It could be a glass of wine, or buying a nice coffee mug.

- **Change Your Inner Voice:** The conversations you have with yourself are the most important. There's no point in other people believing in you if you don't believe in *yourself*. Your thoughts are connected to how you feel, and apathy often involves negative thinking such as, "I might as well not bother; I'll probably fail anyway," or, "I can't get anything right." Instead of dwelling on those thoughts, replace them with something positive such as, "Even if I fail, I'll learn from it and get it right next time," or, "I'll never know unless I try, so I might as well give it a go." To remind yourself to speak kindly to yourself, write positive affirmations on Post-it notes and stick them around your house. Some positive affirmations could be, "I am kind and smart," "I deserve the best in life," or, "My gifts are a blessing to the world."

- **Connect with People:** Now, this is probably the last thing you want to do considering people are the cause of your apathy; however, the more you interact with people, the easier it will become. This doesn't mean opening the door to toxic people. Socialize with the friends and family members who don't drain your energy and bring out the best in you. Start by choosing someone to have a coffee with once a week before moving on to parties and group settings.

Does your dark empath partner seem to want to save everyone except you? That's probably because they've got the savior complex. If you want to know more about it, keep reading.

CHAPTER 18:

DARK EMPATHS AND THE SAVIOR COMPLEX

Despite their evil side, dark empaths are helpful and compassionate by nature—but their partner will rarely see this side of them because they intentionally hide it. I was often left wondering what was wrong with me when I witnessed James go above and beyond the call of duty to help his friends, family members, and co-workers. When he was around other people, he was a completely different person, and that's why everyone loved him so much. People appreciated his willingness to sacrifice and put others' needs before his own. A lot of people seek assistance from dark empaths because they will go the extra mile to rectify others' situations. However, some dark empaths offer to help people who don't want it, who want to work it out themselves or are content in their misery. People who insist on giving this type of unsolicited help suffer from the savior complex.

SAVIOR COMPLEX SIGNS

According to psychologist Dr. Maury Joseph, a person with a savior complex believes they can save the world. On the surface, there doesn't seem to be anything wrong with having such a positive outlook on life, but there are several problems with the savior complex, as you will soon read. The following are some of the main signs indicating that a person suffers from a savior complex:

You Are Solution-Oriented: Problem-solving is a great skill to have; however, some problems don't have an immediate solution, especially those such as grief, trauma, and illness. Saviors are obsessed with fixing things straightaway and are often more concerned with finding a solution to the problem than the person who actually has the problem is. It's all well and good to offer advice, but sometimes the person doesn't want advice—they want comfort.

You Think You're the Solution: Saviors believe they're the only solution to the problem. As far as they're concerned, no one can help but them. They fantasize about rescuing the person in distress and making their life better. Saviors also have a tendency to believe they're superior to the person they're trying to save. This is especially true when they're in a relationship. They are known to take on a parental role and to baby and patronize their significant other.

You Have Ulterior Motives: Saviors are not conscious of their ulterior motives, but they become obsessed with helping others as a form of escapism. They are either running from the problems in their own lives, or their unresolved trauma manifests in an obsessive desire to save others from their distress.

Self-Sabotage: Saviors go above and beyond to help others. This is referred to as "moral masochism." They overextend themselves or sacrifice personal needs to help people who don't *want* help. Saviors sacrifice things such as emotional space, money, and time.

The Consequences of the Savior Complex

A person with a savior complex does more harm than good because their efforts often go to waste. When the person they're trying to rescue doesn't want help, the changes they make will be fleeting. In some cases, they might detect the savior's reluctance to leave the situation alone until it's resolved and will pretend as if they've been successful just to get the savior to leave them alone. But the savior complex has more of a negative effect on the savior. Here is what it can lead to:

Burnout: Being a savior leaves you feeling depleted, drained, and fatigued. You spend so much time trying to resolve other people's problems that you don't have time for yourself. Another element of burnout for dark empaths is that they are intentionally surrounding themselves with the negative energy of the people they are trying to help, which intensifies the burnout.

Feeling Like a Failure: No one has the power to fix another person's problems when that person doesn't want their problems to be fixed. Because you fantasize about making someone else's life better, you keep chasing something that doesn't exist. You won't be able to save this person, because they don't want to be saved. You are basically setting yourself up for constant disappointment, which will ultimately lead to you feeling like a failure.

Negative Emotions: Because you keep repeating the same behaviors and not getting the results you desire, negative emotions take over. These include:

- Anger or resentment towards the people who reject your help

- Frustration with others and yourself
- A sense of having no control

Fractured Relationships: Saviors might think they're being supportive, but those on the receiving end don't see it that way. Springing into action anytime there's a problem is not seen as support. Some people don't need help; they just want someone to listen while they vent or to discuss ideas with. Your friends and family will eventually start resenting you for your lack of support.

HOW TO OVERCOME THE SAVIOR COMPLEX

The savior complex will ruin your life and your relationships if you let it. Therefore, it's important that you put this destructive personality trait to bed as soon as possible. Here are some tips on how to overcome the savior complex:

The Law of Salvation: A good place to start is to accept the law of salvation. The law of salvation states that *we* are the only people we can save, improve, or control. You can extend an olive branch to others by motivating and inspiring them, but you can't make them change. Real transformation comes from within; it happens because that's what we desire. You are in no way capable of saving someone from their personal demons and mistakes. You don't have the ability to transform a person's heart or the way they live their life. So, instead of wasting your time and energy trying to change other people, focus it on changing *yourself*—if that's what you want.

Listen Instead of React: The moment a loved one tells you they have a problem, you are thinking about a solution before they've finished speaking. You may be guilty of cutting them off and telling them what you think they should do. For example, a friend has just had an argument with her boyfriend and she's confiding in you about it. As soon as she says the word *argument*, you immediately instruct her to dump him because you've seen so many relationships end in disaster because the woman was too forgiving. If you'd let her finish, she would have told you that they came to a resolution and she's really grateful for having a boyfriend who's willing to compromise. The next time someone confides in you, listen to everything they've got to say and don't take any action. Instead, offer your emotional support through kind words and compassion. As mentioned, some people don't want help; they need a listening ear and comfort. You'll achieve a lot more being a support system for your loved ones than a savior.

Focus on Yourself: Perfect people don't exist; we've all got work to do on our characters, and dreams to fulfill. Also, when you've got emotional problems, you are not the right person to help others because it would be the blind leading the blind. If two people can't see, they'll end up in a ditch together. Take some time out and think about whether you've got the time and energy to be fixing someone else's life. Ask yourself the following questions:

- Have you fulfilled your dreams?
- Do you consider yourself fully enlightened?
- Do you have emotional battles?

You can't give people what you don't possess. The most effective way to help someone is to lead by example. As much as you might like the sound of your own voice, people are not concerned about what you say; they are concerned about what you *do*. Therefore, if you really want to help people, get *your* house in order first.

Do you wish your dark empath partner would spend more time trying to please you than they do others? Unfortunately, it won't happen until they get to the root of their people-pleasing problem. Keep reading to find out more.

CHAPTER 19:

THE NEED TO PLEASE—DARK EMPATHS' PEOPLE-PLEASING

It makes absolutely no sense that dark empaths are people pleasers, considering how badly they treat their significant others. Except during the love-bombing stage, they make no attempt to go all out for their partners. But when it comes to everyone else, they have this uncontrollable urge to be liked and needed so they'll do anything to please them. I found it incredibly annoying watching James break his back for everyone but me. What made it worse was that I was also a people pleaser, but I would do everything I could to please *him*. It took me three years to learn that I was wasting my time.

People-pleasing involves putting the needs, wants, and desires of others before your own to satisfy the other person. Dark empaths are major people pleasers. One of the main reasons for their people-pleasing tendencies is that they don't like to cause offense. Additionally, because they are so tuned into the needs of others, they often feel it's their duty to help them because they can connect with their feelings on such a deep level. People-pleasing can happen with anyone, but it's most common with friends, family members, romantic partners, and co-workers. Helping people is a good thing;

however, people-pleasing is unhealthy mentally and physically. People pleasers neglect their own needs and end up burned out and exhausted.

In the long run, people-pleasing has a negative effect on your mental health because it chips away at your self-respect, self-esteem, and self-worth. This is especially true when people are continuously benefiting from your kindness but the same kindness is not returned.

It is also important to mention that people-pleasing is a sign of the personality trait of sociotropy. Experts define it as being obsessed with pleasing others and gaining their approval for the sake of maintaining relationships. Additionally, this behavior is also linked to mental health conditions such as:

- Codependency
- Borderline personality disorder (BPD)
- Avoidant personality disorder
- Anxiety or depression

Signs of People-pleasing

If you are not sure whether you're a people pleaser, there are several signs associated with this personality trait. These include:

- You find it hard to say "no."

- When you do say "no," you feel guilty.

- You're overly concerned with what other people think about you.

- You don't feel comfortable expressing your true thoughts and will agree with other people's opinions, even if that's not how you really feel.

- You put the needs of others first and neglect your own.

- You don't have any time for yourself because you're always doing things for other people.

- You accept responsibility for things that have nothing to do with you.

- You avoid offending people by apologizing all the time.

- You are always going out of your way to do things for people because you want them to like you.

- You suffer from low self-esteem.

- You take part in activities you don't enjoy because you want people to like you.

- You don't like turning people down, because you're afraid they'll think you're selfish.

Because of your empath gift, you tune into the feelings of others, which typically makes you a caring and thoughtful individual. People describe you as a generous person who sacrifices their time and resources for others. However, these positive qualities are often accompanied by a tendency to overachieve, poor self-image, the need for control, and you feel stressed and drained most of the time.

THE CAUSES OF PEOPLE-PLEASING

The first step to overcoming people-pleasing is to understand why you do it. It's not solely because you're an empath; there are other factors at play, and these include:

- **Traumatic Experiences:** Traumatic, difficult, or painful experiences can lead to people-pleasing. Those who suffered abuse, whether during childhood or adulthood, may become people pleasers as a form of protection. Subconsciously, they believe they were responsible for the abuse, and that if they are overly kind to everyone, they won't trigger abusive behavior in others.

- **Perfectionism:** Perfectionists want everything in their lives to be perfect, including the way people think and feel about them.

- **Insecurity:** People pleasers are convinced that no one will like them for who they truly are, but believe that if they do and say all the right things, people will like them.

- **Low Self-Esteem:** People with low self-confidence don't value their own needs and desires. Therefore, they seek external validation by doing things for others in the hopes of acceptance and approval.

THE CONSEQUENCES OF PEOPLE-PLEASING

As an empath, it's in your nature to be a loving and caring person. Being compassionate and having a desire to help others is essential for building and maintaining relationships. However, if your only motive for people-pleasing is that you're afraid of not being liked and you want others to like you, people-pleasing can have severe negative consequences. These include the following:

Fake Relationships: Although you think that people-pleasing will get people to like you, it actually has the opposite effect. A person who says yes to everything is looked at with suspicion because, typically, people are not this way inclined. It is in our nature to be selfish and put ourselves first, and so when someone is constantly going out of their way to help others, people question their motives. Additionally, it opens the door for people to take advantage of you. If someone knows you are going to say yes to everything, they'll keep asking for your help. If you do something they don't like, or they just don't like you, they'll talk about you behind your back, but they'll never express their true feelings to your face because they know they may need you in the future. These are generally the people who never call to see how you are, but only call when they need something.

You Are Unsatisfied: When you can't be your true and authentic self, you'll always live an unsatisfied life because deep down, you know people only like you because of what you do for them. You'll find it difficult to grow in character and truly connect with people because you're always hiding who you truly are.

No Willpower: Getting stuff done, even the normal everyday tasks such as going to work and doing the laundry, takes grit and willpower. But when you devote all your mental resources and energy to pleasing others, you won't have anything left for yourself. If your first thoughts when you wake up in the morning involve running down a mental list of everything you need to do for everyone else, you're not putting yourself first. According to research, self-control and willpower are limited resources, which means they eventually run out, and everything that's important to you gets put off until you've got enough energy to do it—which may never happen.

Stress and Anxiety: When people notice that you're willing to go the extra mile without complaining, they'll squeeze every last drop of time and energy out of you, which leads to stress and anxiety.

You'll feel stressed out because you've got so much to do and not enough time to get it done. And you'll feel anxious because you're overly concerned with ensuring that what you're doing is good enough. As mentioned, helping others is a good thing; it actually has several mental health benefits, including giving you a sense of purpose and satisfaction with life. But on the flip side, excess stress and anxiety can have a negative impact on your physical and mental health. Stress is known to lead to conditions such as heart disease and cancer.

Frustration and Anger: Again, helping people can be a rewarding and enjoyable experience. But if you're doing things that you don't really want to do out of obligation, it can cause frustration and anger. Despite the fact that you're trying to please people because you want them to like you, you may also end up harboring resentment towards them because they're expecting too much from you.

HOW TO OVERCOME PEOPLE-PLEASING

People-pleasing is difficult to overcome because it's not as simple as just deciding that you're going to stop being a people pleaser; there are other underlying issues to deal with. It's even more challenging for empaths because they also need to learn how to differentiate between using their empathic gift for the good of humanity, or for the sake of being liked, and battling with people's emotions when they say "no." Here are some tips on how to stop people-pleasing:

Take Baby Steps: It's not wise to make sudden changes because the brain can't handle it and will quickly revert back to old habits. Therefore, taking baby steps is the best way to get started. Not only do you need to retrain *yourself*, you'll also need to retrain the people around you by enforcing your boundaries. Here's how to get started:

- Say no to smaller requests.

- Express your opinion about something not considered controversial.

- Ask for help to complete a small task.

- Say no via text message.

- Practice saying no to salespeople, at restaurants, and when dealing with colleagues.

Tell Them You'll Think About It: People pleasers often feel obligated to say yes immediately because they don't want to come across as indecisive. It's only when they think about it later on or check their schedule that they realize agreeing was a bad idea. But by this point, it's too late to back out, and this leads to feelings of overwhelm and frustration. Instead of saying yes to a request immediately, tell the person you need to think about it and you'll get back to them later. This way, you can decide whether you've got the time and mental capacity to do it. Your thought process should involve asking yourself questions such as:

- Do I really want to do this, or do I want their approval?

- How long will it take to help this person?

- Can I fit it into my schedule?

- Will I feel stressed out if I say yes?

Additionally, research suggests that pausing before answering leads to people making better decisions. As you grow in confidence, you can implement the pause instead of asking for time to think about it.

Create Boundaries: For more on establishing boundaries, go back to Chapter 2. However, being clear about your boundaries is essential if you're going to eliminate people-pleasing. Letting people know how far they can go with you, and what you're willing to do for them will prevent them from taking advantage of you. When they know that you're not going to do it, they'll stop asking. You can also establish boundaries by only being available at certain times. For example, let your friends, family members, and co-workers know that you're not available after 9:00 p.m. because that's when you go to bed. This will stop those who call you at all hours of the morning, and it will also stop people from asking you to do things like pick them up from the airport at 11:00 p.m.

Set Priorities and Goals: Setting concrete priorities and goals and actively working towards them cuts out the non-essentials in your life. When you write your goals down and set a deadline, you prioritize your time and won't be able to help people the way you used to. It also gives you an excuse to say no immediately. When they ask, you can say, "Sorry, I've got to finish writing my book by [deadline date]; I won't be able to do that right now I'm afraid." People are more forgiving when you've got a legitimate reason for saying no. People-pleasing depletes your time and energy. When you set goals, you'll need that time and energy to complete them.

Stop Offering Your Services: Are you the person who always offers to help without being asked? Because empaths can sense when people are in need, they always come to the rescue. You are praised for your ability to do this, which gives you even more of an incentive to continue. As of today, make a promise to yourself that you'll only help when asked, and even then, you won't accept every request. Once you implement this strategy, you'll be surprised at how much extra time you have on your hands.

Ask for Support: No man is an island, and everyone needs help to achieve their goals, so ask friends and family to help you with this. Asking them will be awkward because these are the very people always asking *you* for help. You can definitely expect some tension here, and you'll find out who your real friends are. But even if you have just one person to support you, it will be enough. Ask them to monitor your people-pleasing behavior (they may have already noticed it) and to bring it to your attention when they notice you doing it.

Study Conflict Resolution: People pleasers will do everything in their power to avoid conflict. Therefore, it only makes sense that you familiarize yourself with conflict-resolution strategies so you feel confident handling such situations when they arise. Here are a few tips I've taken from *Crucial Conversations* by Kerry Patterson & Joseph Grenny, a book I highly recommend:

- **Connect with Your Feelings:** Dark empaths find it difficult to connect with their feelings because they're so in tune with everyone else's. But the first step to handling conflict resolution is to connect with your feelings. You might feel resentful or angry, but you can't figure out why. Or you may feel that someone isn't doing what they're supposed to, but you don't know what you want from them. Journaling is a great way to get in touch with your feelings; however, the process can arouse strong emotions you didn't know were there and you may need therapy to deal with them.

- **Active Listening:** A lot of people who ask for your help don't actually need it; they know exactly what to do—they just need someone to tell them. You will detect this in what is said, and oftentimes in what is *not* said. Because dark empaths are compassionate and are good at seeing things from other people's perspectives, they take on problems that are not theirs because they have an innate sense of what needs to be done to resolve issues. Sometimes, before the person has fully expressed themselves, empaths have already come up with a solution. However, when a person feels that you've listened to and understood exactly what they need, it gives them the confidence they need to help themselves. The next time someone asks for help, let them explain themselves properly and repeat back what they've said. It's usually at this point that they realize they don't need you after all.

- **Clear Communication:** Become more assertive when communicating your needs so that everyone knows where they stand. Saying the wrong thing can make the situation worse. Speak your mind in a clear and concise way without being aggressive. You can achieve this by doing the following:

  - **State the Facts:** If a friend is always late, don't say, "I can't stand the fact that you're always late." Instead, say, "We were supposed to meet up at 10:00—it's now 10:30. Can you make more of an effort to be on time, please?"

- **Don't Exaggerate or Judge:** Refrain from judging, exaggerating, or labeling behavior. Again, be factual about what you don't like. Don't say, "Our breakfast is ruined now because you couldn't be on time." Instead, say, "I'll need to shave thirty minutes off our breakfast time because I've got to be back in the office by 11:00."

- **Start with "I":** Start your sentences with "I" instead of "you." When you use the word "you," the person will immediately go into defense mode because it sounds as if you're attacking them or being judgmental. By using the word "I," the focus is on how you feel because of their behavior. Also, it shows that you're not blaming them for how you feel but taking ownership of your feelings. By displaying your ability to take responsibility for your feelings, the person you're dealing with is more likely to mirror you. For example, instead of saying, "You need to stop making me feel so frustrated because of your inability to be on time," instead say, "I feel so frustrated when you're late." Hopefully, this will lead to a discussion because there are most likely some underlying issues going on, which will give you deeper insight into their behavior.

- **Behavior, Results, Feelings:** When confronting the issue, use the "behavior, results, feelings" formula. For example: "When you don't arrive on time, I'm left wondering what's going on, and I feel worried and frustrated."

- **Solution:** Use the win-win strategy to come up with a solution that will benefit the both of you. Because your friend is always late, maybe you can arrange to meet at a place closer to their location. Or you can make plans when your schedule is clear for the day so it won't bother you when they're late. You can bring a book and wait patiently.

Practice Self-Care: People pleasers don't have time for self-care because they're so focused on everyone else that they put themselves last. They are so busy seeking outside validation that they've lost touch with the fact that true validation comes from within. *You are the only person who can improve and maintain your self-esteem, because when it comes from other people, the moment you withdraw it, you're left with nothing.*

Set a weekly appointment for self-care and refuse to break it, no matter how demanding people become. The universe has a funny way of testing how serious you are about your decisions, and the minute you set that appointment, you'll have three people vying for your time on that day. Stand your ground and don't give in. As I keep saying, helping people isn't the problem, but you can't pour from an empty cup. In order to show up as the best version of yourself, you've got to make time to become the best version of yourself.

Don't Give an Explanation: You have the right to say "no" without telling the person why. People pleasers feel they need to over-explain everything when they decline a request because they want to ensure the person fully understands why they can't help, to prevent that person from withdrawing their love. But haven't you noticed that the more you try and explain yourself, the harder they try and convince you otherwise? Don't give them the opportunity to do this. Keep your interaction with them short and sweet. You can say something like, "As much as I'd love to be there for you, that's not something I can take on right now." You don't need to say anything else. The person will probably ask for your reasons, in which case you can say something like, "It's just not something I can do at this time." At this point, you can either walk away, or hang up the phone. You'll feel terrible at first, but the more you stick to your boundaries, the easier it will become.

Be Selective About Who Deserves Your Help: Make a list of the people you're always breaking your back for but don't get any help from them when *you* need it. These are the people you should be the firmest with when it comes to saying no. The good news is that these are also the people who will start walking out of your life once they realize they can't manipulate you anymore.

Do you feel as if no matter what you do, you can't get anything right? That's probably because your dark empath partner is a perfectionist and has a fear of failure but projects their perfectionism onto you. In Chapter 20, you'll get a better understanding of why your partner subjects you to such cruelty.

CHAPTER 20:

PERFECTIONISM AND THE FEAR OF FAILURE

Perfectionism is the desire to be perfect in every area of life. Everyone loves perfectionists, especially in the workplace. A detail-oriented employee who always makes sure their i's are dotted and their t's are crossed is every manager's dream come true. But there are also a lot of negative effects of perfectionism that most people (apart from the perfectionists) are aware of. You see, on the surface, everything looks so wonderful and well put-together, but underneath lies a cesspool of insecurity. A perfectionist has unrealistic standards for themselves, and when they don't meet them, they are highly critical of themselves. In some cases, the extent of the criticism from their inner voice can be compared to emotional abuse. They won't accept anything less than perfection from others, and when others don't meet their standards, the perfectionist becomes very judgmental, critical, and controlling.

Signs of Perfectionism

I am writing about perfectionism because it was one of the things James struggled with. He couldn't go outside unless he was perfectly made up; his clothes had to be immaculate, and everything he touched had to turn to gold or he would beat himself up. Everyone thought he was a genius, but he couldn't see what everyone else saw and only focused on the flaws. The only reason anyone got to read his content was because he worked in marketing and writing was a part of his job. He won several awards for his writing skills, yet he spent years procrastinating before writing his first book because deep down, he felt he wasn't good enough. In case you're wondering whether your dark empath partner is a perfectionist, here are some of the main signs:

Low Self-Esteem: Perfectionists are the opposite to high achievers. High achievers have extremely high self-esteem, whereas perfectionists have extremely low self-esteem. This is because they are constantly criticizing themselves. The most important voice you hear throughout the day is yours. Everyone, including friends, family, and co-workers, was always telling James how good a writer he was. But their affirmations didn't mean anything because he wasn't affirming *himself*. He was too busy comparing himself to award-winning authors and telling himself he was useless. No one convinced him he was incapable of writing a book but himself.

Defensiveness: James couldn't stand constructive criticism because it confirmed what he thought about himself. Unlike high achievers who thrive on constructive criticism because it pushes them to improve their skills, perfectionists take it personally and get defensive. When he received constructive criticism, James was too much of a coward to say anything to his manager's face. He would smile and agree when he critiqued him, but he would go home and spend hours on the phone complaining about it to whoever would listen.

Procrastination: You can read more about procrastination in Chapter 21. It doesn't make sense that perfectionists are prone to procrastination because it defeats the purpose of being a perfectionist. But research suggests that when a perfectionist is unable to adapt to their situation or environment, they resort to procrastination. This is referred to as *maladaptive perfectionism.* Perfectionists are so afraid of failing that they spend all their time and energy worrying about getting it wrong, and they become immobilized and don't do anything at all. This creates a vicious cycle because procrastination makes you feel like an even greater failure. This was the story of James's life before he finally got it together and started writing his book. Year after year, he sank deeper and deeper into depression because he couldn't get started due to his fear of failure, but he would get even more depressed because of all the time he was wasting. He didn't think he would ever make it.

Fear of Failure: Perfectionists have a terrible fear of failure because they spend too much time focusing on the outcome. Their main concern is, "What if I get it wrong?" because if it's not perfect, the perfectionist considers it a failure. This fear prevents them from getting started because they've convinced themselves they'd rather not know the outcome than do it and fail. They find it difficult to accept that there's nothing wrong with failure. The majority of successful people failed several times before getting their big break. There are many lessons in failure—in fact, you learn more from failure than you do from success. Reading autobiographies of highly successful people helped James overcome his fear of failure. Here are just a few people who failed miserably before becoming successful:

- **Steven Spielberg:** Perhaps one of the most famous directors in the world, Steven Spielberg's films have grossed over $9 billion and earned him three Academy Awards, seven Golden Globes, and eleven Emmys. However, the University of Southern California's School of Cinematic Arts rejected him twice. Additionally, he suffers from dyslexia, which made studying difficult for him.

- **Walt Disney:** Despite the fact that Walt Disney died more than fifty years ago, he became so successful during his lifetime that his name lives on through his work today. If Walt Disney had listened to his former newspaper editor, the world would never have been introduced to his work. He was told that he didn't have any good ideas and that he had no imagination. Disney ignored those comments and went on to build the most successful cartoon empire of all time.

- **Abraham Lincoln:** Who would have thought that Mr. Lincoln would go on to become the sixteenth president of the United States with the string of failures he had under his belt? His biggest failure was going to war as a captain and returning as a private (the lowest rank in the military). He attempted to start several businesses, and each one of them failed. Lincoln then decided to try his hand in politics and failed several times before he became president.

- **Stephen King:** King was one of the many authors James compared himself to, believing that he would never achieve their level of success and so there was no point in trying. But while he was so focused on King's credentials, he failed to realize that the renowned author's first book *Carrie* was rejected by thirty publishers! He was told that his type of work didn't sell, so there was no point in putting it out there. He became so dejected that he threw his novel in the trash. His wife fished it out and convinced him to try one last time. He took her advice, and today he's one of the most successful authors of all time.

- **Elvis Presley:** No matter when you were born, you will know of Elvis Presley. But his teachers told him he'd never make it in the music industry, and the first time he performed in a band at the Grand Ole Opry, the leader of the band fired him and told him to go back to his job as a truck driver because entertainment wasn't in his blood. Elvis went on to win several awards throughout his career such as the American Music Award of Merit, the Grammy Lifetime Achievement Award, and the Grammy Award for Best Inspirational Performance.

Depression: As mentioned, perfectionists exist in a never-ending cycle of depression because they never achieve their goals. When things don't go their way, they give up way too easily and then get depressed because of their perceived failure. James was rejected by several publishers before he decided to self-publish. But he eventually learned that rejection was what he needed to push him in the right direction. It's all well and good being published by a traditional publisher, but the publishing industry has changed drastically in recent years, and authors are making more money publishing independently than they are with traditional publishers. Just like Steven King, he was told that the nonfiction niche he was writing in didn't sell. But evidently that wasn't the case because his book sold thousands of copies and he was able to quit his job and write full-time. I doubt he would have realized his full potential if his book had been published by a traditional publisher.

Results-Driven: Perfectionists don't like the process of goal achievement. They are so concerned with hitting their target that they can't enjoy the lessons learned along the way. Perfectionists want to jump from A to Z; they want to see the full manifestation of the vision they have in their mind. Being results-driven was a major problem for James. He was so desperate to become as successful as Steven King that he couldn't appreciate the small strides he was making. There is no such thing as overnight success. Everyone who ever does anything great in life has to go through a process to get there, and when they do finally arrive at their destination, they have an abundance of valuable life lessons to help them continue their journey.

"All or Nothing" Thinking: Almost perfect is considered failure to a perfectionist. When they set a goal and strive for excellence, they expect to achieve excellence. If they don't, it's a problem. For example, coming second place is a no-no for a perfectionist. Despite the fact that they still did an amazing job, they're not concerned about what they've achieved; their focus is on what they *didn't* achieve—which is first place.

THE DANGERS OF PERFECTIONISM

Perfectionism can cause mental health issues. After going through this list, if you feel your perfectionism is leading you to a place from which you don't think you'll be able to get out, it's essential that you seek professional help. Perfectionism can lead to:

- Obsessive compulsive disorder (OCD)
- Suicidal thoughts
- Eating disorders
- Anxiety

- Depression
- Stress
- Burnout

HOW TO OVERCOME PERFECTIONISM

The good news is that you can overcome perfectionism if you want to. James was an extreme perfectionist, but after consistently applying the following strategies, he beat the perfectionism trap. Here are some tips on how to overcome perfectionism:

Become More Self-Aware: If, after reading this chapter, you've come to the conclusion you're a perfectionist, you are already at the first stage of awareness. You can't overcome a problem if you don't acknowledge you have it. Although the aforementioned symptoms are common amongst perfectionists, you are a unique individual with a unique set of issues. Therefore, spend some time reflecting on your perfectionist tendencies. It would help if you wrote them down. Here are a few things to consider:

- What are your thought processes surrounding perfectionism?

- How do you feel when you don't achieve perfection?

- How is perfectionism holding you back from achieving your goals?

- What does failure mean to you?

- How do you handle failure?

- How do you respond to constructive criticism?

These questions will trigger more thoughts and questions. Just keep writing until you feel you can't write anymore. Once you become aware of how perfectionism controls your life, you'll be able to start changing the narrative surrounding it.

Make Room for Mistakes: When you start working on a project, accept that there's a chance you'll make mistakes. When you do make a mistake, you'll realize it's not the end of the world. Learn from it and keep moving. Mistakes are a great way to grow and learn so we can do better. A great way to get over your fear of making mistakes is to learn a new hobby. Choose something you're totally unfamiliar with and dive into it headfirst. You will definitely make mistakes because its new to you, but what you'll find is that the mistakes will teach you how to do it better. The more you practice, the better you'll become at it.

Set Realistic Goals: There's nothing wrong with being a big dreamer. The problem is that when you set unrealistic goals, you set yourself up for failure. When I decided to write a book, I set a ridiculous goal of selling one million copies. You'll feel more confident and a lot less stressed if you set realistic goals.

Eliminate Negativity: Social media was one of James's biggest downfalls. He would spend hours scrolling, comparing his life to influencers and getting depressed because he didn't feel he could compete. The more he scrolled, the more depressed he got and the deeper he fell into procrastination. One of the first things he eliminated when he started writing his book was social media. James disabled all his accounts and deleted them from his home screen. It didn't take long before he realized how problematic social media was. Without them, he immediately felt less anxious, and he could focus more. James did eventually go back to social media simply because it's a good promotional tool, so now, that's exactly what he uses it for: to promote his books and engage with his audience. He logs on three times a week for one hour at a time, and that's it—his scrolling days are over; he doesn't let social media control him, and he is in full control of how he uses it. What negative influences do you have in *your* life that are holding you back? Figure out what they are and eliminate them.

Stop Procrastinating: You can read more about how to stop procrastinating in Chapter 21. Overcoming procrastination is one of the major keys to overcoming perfectionism. When you've got a project to work on, don't overthink it—just start. Don't focus on the end result. Decide that you're going to do one thing every day to complete the project. Breaking the task up into small, manageable chunks is the most effective way to approach it because it's a lot less overwhelming. When James started writing his first book, he only wrote for an hour a day, and he probably wrote about three hundred words at a time. It doesn't sound like much, but what it does is build momentum, and before you know it, you've completed the task.

Focus on Impact: Instead of focusing on perfection, focus on making an impact. It's not always possible to do this as it will depend on what you're working on. James began thinking about all the people he could help by writing books, and that became his motivation. It was bigger than him. This wasn't about becoming a successful author. He wasn't writing for recognition; he was writing to change lives. The more he focused on impact, the less hold perfectionism had over him. Before getting started on something, think about why you're doing it. Once you figure out your *why*, focusing on it becomes a lot easier.

Embrace Criticism: It's a bad idea to be surrounded by "yes people" because you'll never grow. Think about it like this: if you want to transform your body, you've got to go to the gym and lift weights. You can't keep lifting the same weights or your muscles won't grow. To get the results you desire, you've got to push your body to the limit. The same principle applies in life. As a perfectionist, you desire to be the best, but the only way to become the best is to keep making improvements. But how will you know where you need to make improvements if no one tells you? Surrounding yourself with people who tell you how great you are all the time will only cause stagnation. You'll feel good about yourself because your peers are always singing your praises, but you'll remain on the same level. Therefore, get around people who will force you to level up through constructive criticism. When your manager, partner, or a friend tells you where you need to make improvements, thank them and get to work.

Be More Positive: This sounds really cliché, but it's an essential component to overcoming perfectionism. Perfectionists are very negative thinkers; they don't focus on what's good about something, but on what's *wrong* with it, and that includes themselves. A perfectionist can be the most articulate and talented person, but they'll focus on not being tall enough, pretty enough, or intelligent enough. No one else can see the negatives, but to the perfectionist, it's magnified. It's definitely easier said than done, but make a conscious effort to focus on the good stuff about yourself, other people, and your work.

Get Therapy: Finally, if nothing else works, you may need to seek professional help. Sometimes, you just can't do it on your own. Maybe you had a really bad childhood and the trauma you endured is affecting you so badly, you can't move on. There is no shame in seeing a therapist. I've seen one, and many of my friends have too. Not only do they help you put things into perspective, but they provide you with the tools you need to overcome your struggles.

In the final chapter, we will look at why dark empaths have a tendency to procrastinate over everything.

CHAPTER 21:

DARK EMPATHS ARE MAJOR PROCRASTINATORS

We've all heard the saying, "Procrastination is the thief of time." But I'd like to change that to, "Procrastination is the thief of destiny." You see, not doing what you need to do to ensure you arrive at your place of purpose will ensure you do *not* arrive at your place of purpose. You are the only person capable of breathing life into your vision, and if you're not willing to put the work in, you'll never make it. People procrastinate because they're afraid of failure, and they're afraid of who they'll become once they succeed. If you never get started, you can't fail—because you never tried. But if you do make it, you're pushed out of your comfort zone, and that scares a lot of people. When I met up with James again years after the breakup, I asked him if he ever found out the deeper meaning behind his procrastination. He said that during therapy he discovered that he had become so comfortable living life as a dark empath that change frightened him. But he wasn't afraid of becoming better; he was afraid of becoming worse. He was afraid of being further corrupted by success. Procrastination was another hurdle we managed to overcome while we were together, and it was wonderful to watch him accomplish so much. So, in this chapter, I would like to share with you the steps he took to overcome procrastination and become an award-winning author.

ACKNOWLEDGE YOUR PROCRASTINATION

The first step to overcoming procrastination is to acknowledge it. Procrastinators never take accountability for why they don't get stuff done. Instead, they make excuses. For example, you know you've got a deadline to meet but you've chosen to clean out your closet instead. You've convinced yourself that your untidy closet is making you less productive, but the reality is that you're putting off working on the project because you don't want to do it. The minute you sit at your desk with the intention of working on your project but then decide you're going to do something else is a sign that you lack the motivation to complete that specific task. Notice that you have the motivation to clean out your closet? You can now admit that you're procrastinating.

ACKNOWLEDGE YOUR FEAR OF FAILURE

It took James years to start writing books because he was afraid of failing. He knew he had a writing gift, but he was scared it wouldn't be received by the world. Every January, he would make the same new year's resolution to write his first book by the end of the year. By the end of the year, he'd only written half a chapter. He would set himself the task of waking up an hour early to write, but would stay up late talking on the phone or watching TV and then hit the snooze button when the alarm went off. He had convinced himself that his problem was because he wasn't a morning person—when the only reason he couldn't get up was because he went to bed late. After a couple of months of failing to wake up an hour early, he would cancel that and set another task, this time of writing for an hour after work. But the first thing James would do when he got back from work was have dinner in front of the TV and keep telling himself, "Five more minutes." Those five minutes never arrived, and he'd spend the whole night in the same spot on the couch. After a couple of months of failing to write for an hour after work, he'd set another task of writing for five hours over the weekend. As I'm sure you've guessed, that didn't happen either. But the moment he acknowledged his fear of failure, he was able to snap out of the procrastination trap.

James had to evaluate himself and confront the fact that he was afraid his books wouldn't be good enough. That they would sit on Amazon's shelves collecting dust, and all his friends and family would give him every reason why he shouldn't have bothered in the first place. He then had to make a conscious decision not to allow fear to hold him back. He did this by constantly reminding himself of the worst-case scenario, which was that his books wouldn't sell and everyone would laugh at him. Big deal! Was that going to ruin his life? No. On the other hand, if James didn't write the book, he'd never know if he would have been successful and he'd have to live with the pain of regret.

CREATE THE RIGHT ENVIRONMENT

Your environment plays a crucial role in your output and productivity levels, and this is especially true for empaths. Clutter traps negative energy, and since we are so sensitive to it, it affects us more. So, the more untidy your house is, the more drained you feel. When our house was a mess, James and I just assumed we were tired all the time because of energy vampires. No matter how much coffee we drank, we still couldn't get it together. James didn't realize he was contributing to his inability to focus until I started reading about my gift. Things drastically changed for us when we got our house in order. We were clearheaded, we slept better, and we felt less frustrated. We used the KonMari method to get our house in order, and the tips I'm about to give you were taken from her bestselling book *The Life-Changing Magic of Tidying Up*. The KonMari method involves getting your house in order by focusing on minimalism. The approach is based on organizing your belongings by working through them in categories, instead of room by room. The KonMari method starts with six basic rules:

1. Make a commitment to get your house in order.

2. Visualize your ideal lifestyle.

3. Get rid of items and thank each one for serving its purpose.

4. Organize according to category and not location.

5. Maintain order.

6. Ask yourself if the items you're keeping give you joy.

The five categories to organize your items into are:

1. Books

2. Papers

3. Clothes

4. Sentimental items

5. Miscellaneous items

The main focus of the KonMari method is to get rid of items you don't need. The average person doesn't realize how much they hoard things. We have clothes, shoes, kitchen utensils, and much more that we haven't used in years, yet they're taking up space in our homes. When we organized our house, we were amazed at the amount of junk we had kept. We filled two large skips! Here's how to get started:

Step 1: Remove all your items from your wardrobes, drawers, tables, and anywhere else you store things. Place them all in the middle of the floor.

Step 2: Start picking up items one by one and ask yourself if it brings you joy. If the answer yes, put it into its rightful category. If the answer is no, put it into the junk pile.

Step 3: Once you've completed all the categories, start putting the items in their rightful place.

It sounds simple, but trust me, it's a mammoth task. It took us three months to organize our home—but it was worth it. Don't try and do everything all at once; you'll get overwhelmed and give up. Instead, do a little bit each day. Eventually, you'll have your house perfectly organized.

Organize Your Workspace: For those of you who'll be working on a side hustle from home, get your workspace in order. One of the reasons James found it so difficult to start writing was because he didn't have a proper desk. He'd set his laptop up on the dining table with the TV playing in the background. It was literally impossible to focus. But when he organized his workspace, his productivity went through the roof. Here are some tips:

- Choose an area in your home to work. Ideally, it won't be in your bedroom because bedrooms are too cozy and there's too much of a temptation to take a nap. If you've got a spare room then great—James chose a small area under his staircase.

- Buy a desk and a comfortable chair.

- Buy stationery and the items you'll need to complete your tasks.

- Buy a lamp.

- Buy some plants to brighten up the area.

- Use fun push-pins and magnets.

- Buy an inspirational mug.

CHANGE YOUR FOCUS

Whatever you focus on is magnified in your life, and since emotions are energy in motion, dark empaths have plenty of energy. The problem is they focus on the wrong things, which is one of the reasons they struggle so much with procrastination. They can spend hours submerged in depressive thoughts and reflecting on the things that have gone wrong in the past. When they've got a lot to do, they consume themselves with thoughts of how difficult it's going to be to achieve the tasks they've set for themselves. When James was trying to write his first book, his mind was plagued with visions of failure. He felt every emotion connected to imagining how awful the book was going to be. He spent most of his time paralyzed with fear. But things started changing for him once he learned to change his focus. Instead of thinking about a negative outcome, he focused on love, gratitude, and a positive outcome for the book. He focused on the joy he would feel when he became a bestseller and started making enough money to quit his day job. As stated, energy flows where the attention goes; everything James visualized, he is living today. He created his dream life by changing his thoughts. I am in no way suggesting that you can just think your way to success—what I am saying is that your mindset will determine your output. Basically, if you think you can't, you won't do anything. But if you think you can, you'll get to work. Execution is the only way to achieve your goals.

PRACTICE MINDFULNESS TO ELIMINATE FEAR

There is no denying you're afraid of failure. James was too, and it almost stopped him from living his dreams and being where he is today. Fear kept him from having the conversation he needed to have with himself to take the first steps. But it's not about pushing fear to the back of your mind and ploughing through—that's the worst thing you can do. Remember, suppressed emotions will eventually manifest in ways that don't benefit you. Instead of letting fear hold you back, the moment you feel the emotion, do the following:

- Stop, and start taking slow, deep breaths while focusing on your breathing.

- Once you feel yourself calm down, pay attention to your surroundings and take it all in to center yourself and become present.

- What stands out to you the most? Is it the smell of your toast? Or the sound of your air conditioning?

- Chant a mantra about the thing that stands out to you the most. For example, "I can smell the delicious scent of toast and dripping butter." Keep saying it until you are ready to stop.

- Now acknowledge your fear by saying, "I acknowledge that I am afraid right now because of the task I have ahead of me."

- When you feel ready, put the fear to one side and get on with whatever you've got to do.

EVALUATE YOUR PRODUCTIVITY TECHNIQUES

James used to be a productivity junkie; he had all these apps, lists, notepads, and strategies for enhancing your productivity—but he used them to procrastinate. He would spend an hour writing a to-do list, organizing things and doing whatever he felt would improve his productivity, but it was just another form of procrastination. He liked the *idea* of being productive, but he wasn't productive. After evaluating his productivity techniques, James narrowed them down to two. He would write out a to-do list the night before and pin it on his notice board right in front of him so it was the first thing he saw when he sat down at his desk. To work, he used the Pomodoro method. It's an app with a timer and an alarm that allows you to work in 25-minute bursts with five-minute breaks. After four 25-minute bursts, you get a 25-minute break. He found this extremely effective, and with these two methods, his productivity levels went through the roof.

HAVE A DAILY ROUTINE

Human beings are creatures of habit, and their habits either work for or against them. Whether people acknowledge it or not, everyone has a daily routine that typically works against them. James's went something like this:

- Go to bed late.

- Wake up late.

- Have a cup of coffee.

- Rush around getting ready.

- Stop off at McDonald's drive-through for breakfast.

- Eat and drive.

- Get to work just on time.

- Come home from work and watch TV.

He did the same thing Monday to Friday for the two years we were living together. It wasn't until he got dissatisfied with his life and started reading books about how to change it that he realized he was self-sabotaging with bad habits. It took a while to change them—and the catalyst was changing his daily routine. James made slow and intentional changes throughout the year. The first changes looked like this:

- Go to bed and wake up at the same time each day.

- Have a cup of coffee.

- Get ready for work.

- Have breakfast.

- Get to work 30 minutes early.

- Come home from work and watch TV.

To get started, the only thing he changed was going to bed and waking up at the same time each day, and having breakfast at home. He did this for 30 days, and continued for another 30 days, and then another 30 days. He kept track and motivated himself by writing the numbers 1 to 30 on a piece of paper, sticking them next to our light switch, and crossing each day off with a red marker. The benefits James received from making these small changes were astounding. He was less anxious, more productive at work, and he had a lot more energy because he wasn't starting his day eating an unhealthy McDonald's breakfast. The second changes looked like this:

- Go to bed and wake up at the same time each day.

- Have a cup of coffee.

- Get ready for work.

- Have breakfast.

- Get to work 30 minutes early.

- Come home from work and read a book for 30 minutes before watching TV.

James also did this for 90 days, during which time he read five self-help books and made notes of the strategies he was going to implement. The books he read changed his life, and I think they'll do the same for you. The third change looked like this:

- Go to bed and wake up at the same time each day.
- Have a cup of coffee.
- Go for a 15-minute run.
- Get ready for work.
- Have breakfast.
- Get to work 30 minutes early.
- Come home from work and get my house in order for 30 minutes.

He did this for 90 days, and transformed his body and our home. We spoke earlier about the importance of having a clear space. He felt he needed to achieve this before he started working on his goal of writing his first book within a year. The fourth change he made looked like this:

- Go to bed and wake up at the same time each day.

- Have a cup of coffee.

- Go for a 15-minute run.

- Get ready for work.

- Have breakfast.

- Get to work 30 minutes early.

- Come home from work and practice self-care for 30 minutes.

James did this for the last three months of the year, and by the end of December he was a new person. His mind, body, and spirit were stronger, his house was in order, and he was ready to achieve his goal of writing his book within a year. From January 1st, his daily routine looked like this:

- Go to bed and wake up at the same time each day (1 hour, 30 minutes earlier).

- Have a cup of coffee.

- Go for a 15-minute run.

- Get ready for work.

- Have breakfast.

- Write for an hour.

- Get to work 30 minutes early.

- Come home from work and write for two hours.

- Write all weekend.

James surpassed his goal and finished writing his book within six months! He couldn't believe what he had achieved. The book was so successful that within three months of its release, he handed in his notice and started writing full-time. A consistent daily routine helps you build momentum and solidifies good habits. It rewires your subconscious mind so that everything you do is on autopilot. It's no longer a struggle to go to bed and wake up at the same time. James didn't even need to set an alarm; his body automatically let him know when he was tired and when he needed to wake up. It's truly amazing what consistency can do.

MOTIVATION FOR THE LONG TERM

Motivation is a momentary feeling that runs out after a certain time. For example, you can watch a powerful film, listen to someone's success story, or hear a motivational speech and feel ready to take on the world. You'll be on your grind for a few days, maybe even a few weeks, but then you slowly start falling back into your old habits. The only way to keep the momentum going is to motivate yourself daily. Despite the fact that James's mind had been programmed to do things on autopilot, he had plenty of days where he didn't want to do anything, and he had to motivate himself to get started. What really helped him was listening to motivational speeches. He'd turn them on as soon as he'd open his eyes, and he'd listen to them while his drinking coffee, going for a run, getting ready for work and having breakfast. He would also listen to motivational speeches during his lunch breaks. They disrupted his negative thinking pattern and got him into focus mode. When he listened to motivational speeches, he felt more confident and capable, and believed in himself more. One of James's favorite motivational speakers was Les Brown. He had a very difficult upbringing and was labeled a failure as a child because he was diagnosed with educational retardation. He had very low self-esteem and accepted the label he was given. But one teacher believed in him and told him he could do anything he set his mind to. Although Les Brown didn't go to college, he went on to become the most successful motivational speaker in the world. If *he* could conquer his fears to become the most successful motivational speaker in the world, anyone can achieve their dreams.

CELEBRATE YOUR SMALL WINS

As stated, human beings are creatures of habit, and when we're rewarded, we repeat the behavior. When dog owners are training their dogs, they get the dog to perform the behavior, and then reward them. The dog then repeats the behavior because he knows he'll get a reward. The human brain works in the same way. When you're learning a new habit, you can train yourself by rewarding yourself anytime you perform the action. James loved the Pomodoro method for this reason; every two hours, he got a 25-minute break, during which time he would reward himself by watching an episode of one of his favorite shows. Before he started writing his book, he would watch Netflix shows religiously, but the way he watched them was harming his productivity because he would sit in front of the TV all night. But by giving himself something to look forward to after he had completed his tasks, he became more focused. There's nothing wrong with having fun and watching TV, but it becomes a problem when it's not done in moderation and it has control over you. James also gave himself a treat after he'd finished writing each chapter, and that was to watch a movie with a large bowl of sweet popcorn and a packet of peanut sweet treats!

James writing his first book was the beginning of his healing journey. Although we broke up because he wasn't ready to confront his dark side just yet, I still witnessed him achieve the one thing he'd spoken about with passion throughout our relationship. Everything happens for a reason, and I believe James and I had to break up so he could become who he was destined to be. Because we were both unhealed, we held each other back in so many things, and neither of us grew our wings and started to fly until we went our separate ways. But his life today is evidence that dark empaths can change—so don't give up. It may not happen now, but eventually it will if they want it badly enough.

CONCLUSION

get that you want to believe everyone is just as loving, kind, and compassionate as you. But unfortunately, that's not the case. As you've read, dark empaths exist, and they can be pretty nasty. But they can change if they want to. They may have narcissistic tendencies, but they don't suffer from narcissistic personality disorder, so getting the help they need is a lot easier for them. Psychologists have labeled dark empaths as having "the most dangerous personality type." Having had a three-year-long personal relationship with one, I don't believe this is true. I would agree that they're dangerous because they are difficult to spot, but the "most dangerous" label—absolutely not. I think narcissists are far worse; I've dated several narcissists, and not one of them has reformed. On the other hand, James has completely turned his life around, and I'm proud of him. Was he a terrible boyfriend? Absolutely, but when you've got deep-rooted psychological issues you don't know anything about, does it come as a surprise that you're not going to be the nicest person in the world?

To me, dark empaths have been corrupted, and I say this because James was my mirror image. He was equally as affected by other people's emotions as I was, but due to all the pain and trauma in his life, his heart had become so callused, he buried any emotions he felt, including his own. This doesn't take away from the fact that dark empaths make very difficult romantic partners, and if you're looking for a happy and fulfilling relationship, you should avoid them like the plague. Despite the fact that they're difficult to spot, their dark triad personality traits are immediate red flags and you should run in the opposite direction as soon as you detect these. Dark empaths play the game better than narcissists because they have an emotional depth that allows them to keep their manipulative traits under control. It took me a lot longer to realize that James was a dark empath than it did to realize that some of my partners were narcissists.

Recognizing the signs early on will save you from a lot of pain and heartache. But I would say the first sign to look out for is love-bombing. If you've just met someone who professes their undying love for you too soon, don't fall for it. I would also advise that you pay attention to emotional unavailability. Pay attention to their reaction to emotionally sensitive subjects. Do they clam up or try to change the subject? And finally, pay attention to your gut feeling. I believe that, deep down, all humans know when they're going in the wrong direction because their inner man speaks to them. There's an unnerving feeling that something isn't quite right with our partner, but we choose to ignore it because we think we can help them.

Additionally, focus on tapping into your personal power and becoming the best version of yourself. The stronger you are, and the more in tune you are with your instincts and gift, the more the darkness loses its ability to infiltrate and hijack your peace.

THANKS FOR READING!

I really hope you enjoyed this book and, most of all, got more from it than you had to give.

It would mean a lot to me if you left an Amazon review—I will reply to all questions asked!

Simply find this book on Amazon, scroll to the reviews section, and click "Write a customer review".

Or alternatively, please visit www.pristinepublish.com/darkempathreview to leave a review

Be sure to check out my email list, where I am constantly adding tons of value. The best way to get on the list currently is by visiting www.pristinepublish.com/empathbonus and entering your email.

Here, I'll provide actionable information that aims to improve your enjoyment of life. I'll update you on my latest books, and I'll even send free e-books that I think you'll find useful.

Kindest regards,

Judy Dyer

ALSO BY
Judy Dyer

Grasp a better understanding of your gift and how you can embrace every part of it so your life is enriched day by day.

Visit: www.pristinepublish.com/judy

REFERENCES

Bauer, B. D. (2017). *You Were Not Born to Suffer: Overcome Fear, Insecurity and Depression and Love Yourself Back to Happiness, Confidence and Peace.* Van Duuren Media.

Big Think. (n.d.). *'Dark empaths': how dangerous are psychopaths and narcissists with empathy?*

Cure, E. J. (2022). *Dark Empath: The Intriguing Psychology of the Most Dangerous Personality Type. How to Spot Subtle Dark Triad Traits in People Around You, Set Healthy Boundaries, and Protect Your Energy.* Independently Published.

Freedom, J. (2019). *Overcome Anxiety: A Complete Guide for Manage Anxiety, Manage Worry, Stop Panic Attacks, Overcome Depression. The New Way for A Happy Life.*

King, P. (2018). *Stop People Pleasing: Be Assertive, Stop Caring What Others Think, Beat Your Guilt, & Stop Being a Pushover (Be Confident and Fearless).*

Lmft, M. K. M. (2019). *The Codependency Recovery Plan: A 5-Step Guide to Understand, Accept, and Break Free from the Codependent Cycle.* Althea Press.

MacKenzie, J., & Thomas, S. (2019). *Whole Again: Healing Your Heart and Rediscovering Your True Self After Toxic Relationships and Emotional Abuse.* TarcherPerigee.

Orloff, J. (2018). *The Empath's Survival Guide: Life Strategies for Sensitive People* (Reprint). Sounds True.

Patterson, K., Grenny, J., McMillan, R., & Switzler, A. (2022). *Crucial Conversations and Crucial Confrontations Value Pack by Kerry Patterson (2005-05-03)* (1st ed.). The McGraw-Hill Companies.

Ph.D, S. G. J. (2018). *Cognitive Behavioral Therapy Made Simple: 10 Strategies for Managing Anxiety, Depression, Anger, Panic, and Worry.* Althea Press.

Psychology Today (n.d.). *Introducing the Dark Empath | Psychology Today United Kingdom.*

Sirois, F. M., & Pychyl, T. A. (2016). *Procrastination, Health, and Well-Being.* Elsevier Gezondheidszorg.

Stillman, J. (2022). *New Research: Beware 'Dark Empaths,' the Toxic Personality Type That Hides in Plain Sight.* Inc. Australia.

Sumich, A. and Heym, N. (n.d.). *'Dark empaths': how dangerous are psychopaths and narcissists with empathy?* The Conversation.

The Dark Empath Personality Merges Empathy With Dark Triad Traits—And That Spells Trouble. (2020). *Well+Good.*

Verywell Mind. (n.d.). *Is There Such a Thing as a Worst Personality Type?*

Made in the USA
Monee, IL
08 April 2023